THE
ETHNIC
VEGETARIAN

THE
ETHNIC
VEGETARIAN

TRADITIONAL

and

MODERN RECIPES

from

AFRICA, AMERICA,

and the

CARIBBEAN

ANGELA
SHELF MEDEARIS

author of
IDEAS FOR ENTERTAINING FROM THE AFRICAN-AMERICAN KITCHEN

RODALE

© 2004 by Angela Shelf Medearis

Africa map © Bridgeman Art Library/Getty Images
Double Map of the World © Pat LaCroix/Getty Images
Early North America map © Bettmann/CORBIS
Florida and Cuba map © CORBIS
North United States map © Fototeca Storica Nazionale/Getty Images
Seventeenth Century Atlas of North and South America © PictureQuest
United States map © Jennifer Thermes/Getty Images
Illustration by Cathy Ann Johnson

The Nelson Mandela quote on page 41 is reprinted from his book *Long Walk to Freedom*, which was published by Little, Brown and Company, 1994.
The Vegetarian Diet Pyramid on page 230 is reprinted with permission of Oldways Preservation & Exchange Trust, www.oldwayspt.org.

Library of Congress Cataloging-in-Publication Data

Medearis, Angela Shelf.
    The ethnic vegetarian : traditional and modern recipes from Africa, America, and the Caribbean / Angela Shelf Medearis, author of Ideas for Entertaining from the African-American Kitchen.
          p.   cm.
    Includes index.
    ISBN 1–57954–618–8 paperback
    1. Vegetarian cookery.   2. Cookery, African.   3. Cookery, American.   4. Cookery, Caribbean.   I. Title.
TX837.M494   2004
641.5′636—dc22   2004011010

Distributed to the trade by Holtzbrinck Publishers

2   4   6   8   10   9   7   5   3   1   paperback

FOR my sweet husband,

Michael, my dinner companion

for the past 29 years, thank you for

tasting recipes and typing recipes,

but most of all, thank you for your

love and support.

CONTENTS

ACKNOWLEDGMENTS

Thank you to my sister, Marcia Orlandi, my nephew, Kenneth Prosser, and my friends Jerome Gill and Whitney Swift for their cheerful clerical assistance and their humor and support.

Thank you to Willie Jackson and everyone at the Austin Public Library, Will Hampton Branch at Oak Hill, for their research assistance.

Thank you to Jim and Jeanette Larson for introducing me to vegetarian cooking and resources. Bon appétit, y'all!

INTRODUCTION

ONE MORNING LAST SEPTEMBER, AS I WAS BUSY putting the finishing touches on this book, I set a few heirloom tomatoes from my garden on my kitchen counter — they were going to be perfect in the salad I was planning for lunch. But when I came back to the kitchen, I discovered my granddaughter had eaten them all for breakfast!

"I was only going to eat one," she explained. "But they were so delicious, I couldn't stop myself." I just laughed because I know how tempting a freshly picked tomato is!

I've written this cookbook in the hope that you'll find the recipes just as irresistible as my granddaughter found that tomato.

As for the rest of my family, adding vegetarian dishes to our lives has led us to become more adventuresome eaters. And as our tastes have expanded, we've become more enlightened about the many cultures that are part of our heritage.

To create this cookbook, I gathered recipes from family, friends, and my own collection that reflect my African, African-American, and Native American ancestry. I carefully combined and refined those recipes—and discovered new ones along the way—to create a unique collection of vegetarian recipes with a decidedly ethnic flair. Now that I can share my recipes with you, I invite you to become an ethnic vegetarian.

There are many reasons you might want to explore ethnic vegetarianism. If you're among the many African-Americans who face health issues such as obesity, high blood pressure, heart disease, cancer, or diabetes, vegetarianism may help you address or prevent such illnesses. Vegetarians tend to have lower rates of high blood pressure and heart disease because the food they eat contains less fat and cholesterol. And a vegetarian diet rich in important nutrients, such as antioxidant vitamins, dietary fiber, and minerals has beneficial effects on diabetes, obesity, and some forms of cancer.

You might choose to explore ethnic vegetarianism as a way to embrace your heritage and enjoy the foods your ancestors ate. Some people are surprised to learn that Africans and African-Americans have a long tradition of vegetarianism. A diet rich in fruits, grains, and vegetables helped our ancestors survive the hardships of slavery, antebellum life, the Great Depression, and other hard times with little money.

Or you might choose to become a vegetarian for religious reasons, as many Africans and African-American have. Restrictions against eating meat during certain holy days, against eating pork and certain types of fish and shellfish, and against using processed sugar and flour are a few of the religious dietary laws observed among many ethnic groups.

Generations of Africans and African-Americans have created a wonderful vegetarian cuisine that has gone undocumented and unrecognized in most cookbooks. I've even come across "global" vegetarian cookbooks that fail to include any recipes from Africa. For these reasons and more, I created *The Ethnic Vegetarian* to preserve and showcase my ancestors' vegetarian legacy.

How do you go about becoming an ethnic vegetarian? When I decided to write this book, my husband, Michael, jokingly suggested that I become a vegetarian mathematically: Each week add one *new* ingredient and subtract one *old* ingredient. "Before you know it," Michael said, "you'll be a total vegetarian."

I think his plan is a good one. Taking the suggestions in this book one step at a time will help ease you into a lifestyle and method of cooking that may at first seem unfamiliar. Plus, if you've decided to take this path because you want to eat healthier and take better care of yourself, a gradual change may guarantee you more success than a radical one. I've found that changing my lifestyle slowly, using recipes that retain the essence of foods I remember from my childhood, has helped ease me into my new way of life.

As you move into *your* new way of life, let this book take you on a journey through time and across continents—it's filled with stories and recipes to help you do just that.

The first section, African Vegetarian Recipes, presents a collection of deliciously fortifying dishes from my ancestral homeland, where a vegetarian diet is a natural extension of the African way of life.

Turning to the second section, Afro-Caribbean Vegetarian Recipes, you follow the path of the millions of African captives who were taken to the Caribbean islands to labor as slaves on the region's vast sugarcane plantations.

As is the case in many African-American families, my ethnic identity is strongly influenced by the Native American experience. In the third section of this book, African-American and Native American Vegetarian Recipes, you'll find recipes that reflect direct intersections of our cultures that date back to the colonial times.

As our journey continues, we savor the influence that African cooking had on various North American cuisines. The fourth section of this book delves into Louisiana's renowned Creole and Cajun cuisines—two of the world's most distinctive cooking styles.

The fifth section of the book, Southern Vegetarian Recipes, highlights the influence that African cooks had on many Southern classics. It's fascinating to see how many traditional African recipes were adapted with Southern ingredients. Consider Southern-Style Mustard Greens and Black-Eyed Peas: The combination is pure Southern and yet steeped in African tradition.

Finally, in the last recipe section of this book, Modern African-American Vegetarian Recipes, you'll find everything from Collard Greens Quiche (quiche with a Southern drawl) to Soul Sushi (sushi made from three African ingredients rolled up in a distinctly American way), and a number of other inventive dishes that combine the very best of the culinary traditions that have come before—African, Caribbean, Native American, Creole, and Cajun—to create a new cuisine: Ethnic Vegetarian.

Following the recipes in this book, you'll find ethnic vegetarian menus for all occasions.

At the very end of the book, I've included a handy reference section. Here's where you'll find helpful advice on stocking your kitchen, basic preparation instructions, and a few indispensable recipes including Rich Vegetable Broth, Vegetarian Worcestershire Sauce, and Italian Seasoning Mix. Also included in the reference section are some helpful guidelines for vegetarian health and nutrition.

The Ethnic Vegetarian is not a cookbook for cowards. You'll need an open mind and an adventurous palate to absorb the radical combinations of history, heritage, and flavor that you'll find in these pages. If I can hope for a true sign of success with this book, it would be that some of these recipes become your family's favorites—that together we extend our long, proud legacy of exquisite vegetarian cuisine.

Welcome to the ethnic vegetarian life!

AFRICAN VEGETARIAN RECIPES

I RECALL MY INTRODUCTION TO AFRICAN cooking as a trial by fire. One winter my family was fortunate enough to have a houseguest from Ghana who graciously offered to cook dinner for us. She made palaver, a wonderful stew rich with spinach and peppers that filled our house with mouthwatering spicy aromas.

Perhaps that last detail helps explain why I found out the hard way that palaver also means "trouble." I simply couldn't wait to try the stew. Before my guest could explain, I put a generous spoonful in my mouth. Suddenly, a searing heat shot from my lips to the back of my throat, and within a split second I felt like my head was on fire. After that, my Ghanian friend made sure to show me how to control the heat of a dish by removing the seeds from the peppers before cooking, and I quickly fell in love with African food.

I find African cooking especially appealing for its emphasis on natural ingredients, as well as the simple, delicious flavors that result. And I've also come to regard Africans as the original ethnic vegetarians. Within Africa's many cultures, fruits, grains, and vegetables have always played a vital role in highly adaptable and ever-evolving cooking styles. One of the more obvious reasons why meatless meals are common is because meat is quite expensive and sometimes hard to come by. People in rural areas typically grow their own fruits and vegetables and usually reserve meat dishes for special celebrations; even then it is more commonly served as part of a soup or stew rather than in large quantities.

The sampling of African recipes that follows feature many familiar foods that most Americans may never have realized are native to Africa—leafy greens including spinach, black-eyed peas, chickpeas (garbanzo beans), kidney beans and lentils, eggplant, cucumbers, garlic, onions, okra, sesame seeds, peanuts, watermelon, pumpkin, dates, figs, and coconut. Other ingredients and some of the spicy seasonings may be less familiar to you. Have no fear—enjoy these deliciously unique recipes from Africa's splendidly varied vegetarian table!

▪ CONDIMENTS, APPETIZERS, AND SALADS ▪

▪ SOUPS AND STEWS ▪

▪ MAIN DISHES ▪

■ BREADS AND DESSERTS ■

■ BEVERAGES ■

AFRICAN-STYLE CURRY POWDER

Curry powder is a reflection of the Indian influence on some African recipes. It can be purchased commercially; however, most African and Indian cooks blend their own spices. African curry powder includes more pepper than the traditional Indian blends.

1	tablespoon ground cumin
1	tablespoon ground coriander
1	tablespoon ground turmeric
1½	teaspoons ground ginger
1½	teaspoons ground allspice
1½	teaspoons garlic powder
½	teaspoon cayenne pepper
½	teaspoon chili powder

Combine all ingredients in a bowl. Store in an airtight container in a cool, dry place.

CHERMOULA SAUCE

MAKES ABOUT ¾ CUP

This garlic-infused sauce is popular in Morocco as a marinade for fish and seafood. It's also a wonderful sauce for fresh, roasted, or grilled vegetables.

4	cloves garlic, peeled
1	teaspoon salt
⅔	cup fresh cilantro, finely chopped
⅓	cup parsley, finely chopped
1½	teaspoons sweet paprika
½	teaspoon ground cumin
⅛	teaspoon cayenne pepper
2	tablespoons freshly squeezed lemon juice
¼	cup olive oil

Place the garlic and salt in a food processor and process to combine. Add the cilantro, parsley, paprika, cumin, pepper, and lemon juice. Process for 1 minute. Add the oil and process for another minute.

CUCUMBER AND PEPPER RELISH

MAKES 2 CUPS

Cucumbers are native to central Africa. This tangy relish is a popular condiment in Tunisia and is usually served with couscous.

1 tablespoon freshly squeezed lime juice
1 teaspoon salt
⅛ teaspoon cayenne pepper
2 medium cucumbers, sliced lengthwise, seeded, and cut into 2-inch pieces
2 green bell peppers, seeded, ribs removed, and cut into 2-inch pieces

Combine the lime juice, salt, and cayenne pepper in a medium bowl. Add the cucumbers and bell peppers to the juice mixture. Toss to coat the pieces with the juice mixture. Wrap the bowl tightly with plastic wrap. Marinate at room temperature for at least 8 hours before serving.

TAHINI

MAKES 1½ CUPS

Sesame seeds are native to Africa. They were traded throughout the continent and the Eastern world as early as 2000 B.C. This flavorful condiment is high in calcium and protein. It is delicious in sauces and dressings or as a snack spread on cucumbers, pita bread, or crackers.

¾ pound sesame seeds, toasted
¼ cup peanut oil
¼ teaspoon salt

Place the toasted sesame seeds in a food processor. Add 2 teaspoons of the oil to the bowl and process on high for 30 seconds. Add 3 tablespoons of the remaining oil to the bowl and process for 2 minutes, or until smooth. Add the salt and pulse for a few seconds. If the mixture is a smooth paste, omit the remaining 1 teaspoon oil. If the oil is needed, add and process for another 30 seconds. Scrape the paste into an airtight container and refrigerate.

Cooking Tip: Tahini will keep in a covered glass container for several weeks in the refrigerator. If the oil separates from the paste, just stir before using.

EGYPTIAN CHICKPEA SESAME SPREAD

This spread is also called hummus. The addition of the sesame seeds adds protein, amino acids, calcium, and phosphorus as well as a bit of history to this appetizer. Sesame, called benne *in the Wolof dialect, is probably one of the oldest plants grown for oil and was introduced to the New World by African slaves. Most people serve this on pita bread, but since I'm a Texan, I usually spread it on a flour tortilla and roll it up for a quick snack.*

1	can (15 ounces) chickpeas, rinsed and drained
5	cloves garlic, peeled
2	tablespoons freshly squeezed lemon juice
2	teaspoons sesame seeds
1	teaspoon ground cumin
1	teaspoon salt
1	teaspoon freshly ground black pepper
2	tablespoons olive oil
6	pita bread rounds, sliced in half

Preheat the oven to broil.

Place the chickpeas and the garlic in a food processor or blender and process until smooth. Add the lemon juice, sesame seeds, cumin, salt, and pepper. Process for 1 minute to blend the ingredients.

Brush the oil onto the pita bread. Slice the bread into triangles. Toast the pita bread for 1 minute, or until lightly browned. Serve with the chickpea puree.

PLANTAIN APPETIZER

Plantains are the fruit of a type of banana plant. They are often called "potatoes of the air" or "cooking bananas" because of their similarity in taste and texture to potatoes. When fully ripe, plantains turn from green to yellow to black and become sweeter in flavor. Unlike bananas, plantains must be cooked before being eaten. This dish is called kelewele *in Ghana and is popular as a breakfast dish. I like to serve it as an appetizer as well.*

6	large green plantains, peeled
2	cups vegetable oil
2	tablespoons water
1	teaspoon ground ginger
1½	teaspoons salt
½	teaspoon cayenne pepper

Slice the plantains at an angle to produce longer, larger slices, about 2 inches each.

Heat the oil in a deep skillet over medium-high heat until hot but not smoking.

Combine the water, ginger, ½ teaspoon of the salt, and the pepper in a small bowl. Drop the plantain slices into the ginger mixture. Coat each slice evenly. Shake off any excess liquid and drop the slices into the hot oil. Fry until the slices are golden brown. Remove from the oil with a slotted spoon to a paper towel–covered plate to drain. Sprinkle with remaining 1 teaspoon salt. Serve hot.

BEAN SCOOPS (ACARAJE, AKARA BALLS, BINCH AKARA, KOSAI, KOOSE, OR KWASI)

MAKES 8 SERVINGS

This dish is known by a variety of names in West Africa. The recipe also traveled with the African captives to South America. The traditional recipe calls for removing the skin of the black-eyed peas by soaking them overnight, then rubbing them between your fingers until the skin slips off. These days, I recommend simply grinding the dry peas whole. You retain more nutrients and save time. Bean Scoops are often sold by street vendors who use a slotted spoon to scoop the flavorful snack right out of the hot oil.

1½	cups dried black-eyed peas
½	cup warm water
1	egg
½	teaspoon chili powder
½	teaspoon salt
½	teaspoon freshly ground black pepper
1	medium yellow onion, peeled and grated
2	cups peanut oil

Place the peas in a food processor or blender and process for 3 minutes. Gradually add the water until the mixture turns into a paste. Scrape the bean paste into a bowl and whisk for 5 minutes to aerate the mixture. Add the egg, chili powder, salt, and pepper. Whisk again until the mixture is smooth. Stir in the onion.

Heat the oil in a deep-fryer or deep skillet over medium-high heat until hot but not smoking. Place heaping tablespoons of the bean paste in the oil. Fry the bean mixture for 3 minutes, or until golden brown. Remove from the oil with a slotted spoon to a paper towel–covered plate to drain.

Cooking Tip: For an interesting variation called *Akara Awon*, stir 1½ cups finely minced okra into the bean mixture.

SAMBUSAKS

The combination of feta and Parmesan cheese is what makes these North African pastries taste so delightful. Sambusaks *are delicious hot or at room temperature.*

- ½ cup melted butter
- ½ cup vegetable oil
- ½ cup hot water (120 to 130 degrees)
- ⅛ teaspoon salt
- 3 cups whole wheat or all-purpose flour
- 10 ounces feta cheese, crumbled
- ½ cup grated Parmesan cheese
- 3 eggs
- 2 teaspoons baking powder
- ¼ teaspoon freshly ground black pepper
- 1 tablespoon water

Place the butter, oil, water, and salt in a food processor or large bowl. Process or mix with an electric mixer on medium speed until blended. Add 2 cups of the flour and process or mix until a soft dough forms. Scrape the dough out onto a lightly floured board. Knead the dough, adding in the remaining 1 cup flour a handful at a time. Shape the dough into a ball and wrap it in plastic wrap. Refrigerate for 30 minutes.

Meanwhile, place the feta, Parmesan, 2 of the eggs, the baking powder, and pepper in a food processor or large bowl. Process or mix with an electric mixer on medium speed until light and creamy.

Preheat the oven to 375 degrees. Divide the dough into 20 balls. Using a floured board, flatten each ball into a 4-inch circle with the palm of your hand. Place a rounded tablespoon of the filling in the center of each circle of dough. Brush the edges of the dough with water. Fold the dough over the filling. Seal the edges of the dough by pressing together with the tines of a fork.

Place the finished pastry 2 inches apart on a lightly greased baking sheet. Combine the remaining egg and the water in a small bowl. Brush the top of the pastries with the beaten egg. Bake for 35 minutes, or until golden brown.

GHANAIAN SALAD

MAKES 10 SERVINGS

This is an updated version of a popular West African layered salad. It is almost a complete meal in a bowl. One of the main ingredients is sweet potatoes, which are commonly—and mistakenly—equated in America with yams. Some food historians believe that this misconception may stem from the substitution of the sweet potato for the African yam in name and use by slave cooks in America.

1	large purple onion, peeled and thinly sliced
1	medium cucumber, sliced
1	can (15 ounces) French-style green beans, drained
½	cup red wine vinegar
2	teaspoons salt
1½	teaspoons freshly ground black pepper
¼	teaspoon sugar
3	cups water
½	pound snow peas, strings removed
4	ounces silken, soft tofu, drained
1	cup plain soy milk
2	cloves garlic, peeled and minced
⅛	teaspoon cayenne pepper
1	can (20 ounces) baked beans
4	medium tomatoes, sliced
1	can (15 ounces) whole kernel corn, drained
1	avocado, peeled and sliced
1	can (15 ounces) sweet potatoes, drained and sliced
3	hard-cooked eggs, peeled and sliced

Place the onion, cucumber slices, and green beans in a bowl. Pour the vinegar over the vegetables. Add $\frac{1}{2}$ teaspoon of the salt, $\frac{1}{2}$ teaspoon of the black pepper, and the sugar and toss lightly to coat. Marinate at room temperature for 30 minutes. After 30 minutes, drain the onion mixture in a colander.

Bring the water to a boil in a medium pot over high heat. Add $\frac{1}{2}$ teaspoon of the remaining salt and the snow peas. Reduce the heat to medium and boil for 1 to 2 minutes, or until the peas turn a bright shade of green. Drain the peas in a colander. Place the colander of peas in a bowl of ice water to retain the color and stop the cooking. Drain, shake dry, and set aside.

Combine the tofu, soy milk, garlic, cayenne pepper, the remaining 1 teaspoon salt, and the remaining 1 teaspoon black pepper in a small bowl.

Alternate layers of the baked beans, snow peas, onion mixture, tomatoes slices, corn, avocado, sweet potatoes, and egg with the tofu mixture in a large salad bowl. Press the mixture down with the back of a spoon or a spatula until it is smooth and compact. Cover with plastic wrap and refrigerate for 1 hour before serving.

Cooking Tip: This salad can be prepared in advance and kept in the refrigerator for 2 to 3 days.

NORTH AFRICAN ORANGE SALAD

MAKES 8 SERVINGS

I love the texture and taste of this salad. It makes a wonderful addition to a summer-time meal. A key ingredient here is oranges. Wild oranges were found in Senegambia as early as the mid-fifteenth century by Portugese travelers.

DRESSING

- ½ cup freshly squeezed lemon juice, strained
- 1 teaspoon salt
- ¼ teaspoon cayenne pepper
- 1 cup virgin olive oil

SALAD

- 4–6 handfuls mixed salad greens (romaine or iceberg), trimmed
- 1 large purple onion, peeled and thinly sliced
- 16 Greek olives, pitted and chopped
- 2 large oranges, peeled and thinly sliced

To prepare the dressing: Whisk the lemon juice, salt, and pepper together in a medium bowl. Continue to whisk while slowly adding the oil. Refrigerate until ready to use.

To prepare the salad: Gently toss the salad greens, onion, and olives in a large salad bowl. Arrange the orange slices on top. Drizzle the dressing on top of the salad.

LENTIL SALAD

MAKES 4 SERVINGS

This is a popular main-dish salad during Lent in many parts of North Africa, where meat is not served in observance of the religious season.

½   pound dried lentils, cooked according to package directions, or 1 can (15 ounces) lentils
3   tablespoons red wine vinegar
1   teaspoon salt
½   teaspoon freshly ground black pepper
⅛   teaspoon cayenne pepper
3   tablespoons olive oil
1   medium purple onion, peeled and thinly sliced
1   medium bell pepper, seeded, ribs removed, and sliced

Place the lentils in a colander. Rinse the beans and set aside to drain.

Combine the vinegar, salt, black pepper, and cayenne pepper in a medium bowl. Whisk in the oil. Add the lentils, onion, and bell pepper. Toss the ingredients to coat with the vinegar mixture. Cover the bowl and let the salad marinate at room temperate for at least 1 hour. Stir every 15 minutes to blend the ingredients.

EAST AFRICAN PEANUT SOUP

MAKES 8 SERVINGS

Adding peanuts for protein and grinding nuts to thicken soups and stews is a stan-dard cooking method in Africa. The peanut butter adds a unique taste and richness to this updated version of the traditional African soup.

2	tablespoons olive oil
2	tablespoons butter
4	ribs celery, sliced
2	medium carrots, peeled and sliced into rounds
1	medium yellow onion, peeled and chopped
¼	cup uncooked long-grain white rice
½	teaspoon salt
⅛	teaspoon cayenne pepper
3	cups vegetable broth
½	cup smooth peanut butter

Heat the oil and butter in a large pot over medium-high heat. Add the celery, carrots, and onion. Sauté for 10 minutes, stirring occasionally. Add the rice, salt, and pepper and sauté for 5 minutes. Stir in the vegetable broth. Bring the mixture to a boil over high heat. Reduce the heat to low, cover, and simmer for 20 minutes, or until the rice is tender.

Ladle out 1 cup of the soup broth and place it in a small bowl. Add the peanut butter. Stir until the peanut butter liquefies. Pour the peanut butter mixture back into the soup. Cover and simmer for another 10 minutes.

PLANTAIN AND CORN SOUP

This soup calls for yellow plantains. Using the plantains in this "in-between" ripe stage (no longer unripe and green, not yet fully ripe and black) adds a special richness to the soup.

2	tablespoons peanut oil or vegetable oil
2	tablespoons butter
1	large yellow onion, peeled and chopped
4	cloves garlic, peeled and minced
1	serrano or jalapeño chile pepper, stemmed and sliced (wear plastic gloves when handling)
5	cups vegetable broth
2	teaspoons salt
1	teaspoon freshly ground black pepper
1	pound yellow plantains, peeled and sliced
1	cup fresh or frozen and thawed corn kernels
1	can (28 ounces) peeled whole tomatoes, crushed
½	teaspoon sugar

Heat the oil and butter in a large Dutch oven or pot over medium-high heat. Add the onion. Sauté for 8 to 10 minutes. Add the garlic and chile pepper and sauté for 5 minutes. Add the vegetable broth, salt, and black pepper. Reduce the heat to low, cover, and simmer for 5 minutes. Add the plantains, corn, tomatoes (with juice), and sugar. Cook for 15 minutes, or until the plantains are tender.

EAST AFRICAN TOMATO SOUP

MAKES 8 SERVINGS

This is a great cold soup for a hot summer day. It's even better when prepared a day ahead to give the flavors a chance to blend.

2	cans (28 ounces each) peeled whole tomatoes
1	cup sour cream
½	cup plain soy milk
3	tablespoons freshly squeezed lemon juice
2	tablespoons tomato paste
1	tablespoon olive oil
3	tablespoons chopped parsley
1½	teaspoons salt
½	teaspoon freshly ground black pepper
¼	teaspoon cayenne pepper
½	teaspoon sugar
1	small cucumber
1	ripe avocado

Place the tomatoes (with juice), ⅔ cup of the sour cream, the soy milk, lemon juice, tomato paste, oil, parsley, salt, black pepper, cayenne pepper, and sugar in a food processor or blender. Process to combine. Pour the tomato mixture into a large bowl. Cover the bowl with plastic wrap and refrigerate the soup for at least 2 hours or overnight.

Peel the cucumber and slice it lengthwise in half. Scoop out the seeds by running the tip of a teaspoon down the center of each half. Chop the cucumber into small pieces.

Peel the avocado and chop it into small pieces. Place equal portions of the cucumber and avocado pieces into 8 servings bowls. Pour the tomato soup into the bowls. Place a spoonful of the remaining ⅓ cup sour cream on top of each serving.

Cooking Tip: You can use any variety of avocado for this recipe for equally tasty results. The most popular kind is the Hass avocado. Just a few of the other varieties available include Fuerte, Ettinger, Nabal, and Anaheim.

PEPPER STEW

MAKES 8 SERVINGS

Chile peppers are a common ingredient in African recipes. I especially like this combination of piquant spices with the tomatoes and the collard greens. It infuses the stew with a wonderful flavor.

2	tablespoons peanut oil or vegetable oil
2	tablespoons butter
1	large yellow onion, peeled and diced
4	cloves garlic, peeled and minced
1 or 2	serrano chile peppers, stemmed and sliced (wear plastic gloves when handling)
½	teaspoon ground cumin
½	teaspoon ground cloves
½	teaspoon ground cinnamon
⅛	teaspoon cayenne pepper
1	can (28 ounces) peeled whole tomatoes
1	can (15 ounces) chickpeas, rinsed and drained
6	cups vegetable broth
2	red potatoes, scrubbed and chopped
2	medium carrots, peeled and cut into rounds
2	bell peppers, seeded, ribs removed, and chopped
½	pound collard greens, trimmed and chopped
½	tablespoon salt

Heat the oil and butter in a large Dutch oven or pot over medium-high heat. Add the onion, garlic, chile pepper, cumin, cloves, cinnamon, and cayenne pepper. Sauté for 5 minutes, stirring frequently. Add the tomatoes (with juice), chickpeas, and vegetable broth. Cover and bring the mixture to a boil over high heat.

Reduce the heat to low. Add the potatoes, carrots, bell peppers, collard greens, and salt and simmer for 20 to 30 minutes, or until the vegetables are tender.

SPINACH STEW

MAKES 6 SERVINGS

This stew is popular in Ghana and is quick to prepare.

1	cup pumpkin seeds, shelled and toasted
¼	cup water
¾	cup vegetable oil
1	small yellow onion, peeled and chopped
1	small tomato, sliced
½	cup tomato paste
1	pound fresh spinach, cleaned and chopped, or 1 package (10 ounces) frozen chopped spinach, thawed and squeezed dry
½	teaspoon cayenne pepper
1	teaspoon salt
1½	cups uncooked long-grain white rice

Place the pumpkin seeds and water in a food processor or blender and process until a smooth paste forms.

Heat the oil in a large skillet or pot over medium-high heat. Add the onion. Sauté for 2 minutes, or until golden brown and soft. Add the pumpkin seed paste, tomato, tomato paste, spinach, pepper, and salt. Stir to combine. Reduce the heat to low, cover, and simmer for 30 minutes.

Meanwhile, prepare the rice according to package directions. Serve the stew over the rice.

AFRICAN-STYLE STUFFED BELL PEPPERS

MAKES 4 TO 6 SERVINGS

This savory recipe is a wonderful combination of flavors and an attractive main dish.

½	cup couscous
1	cup boiling water
2	teaspoons salt
8	red or green bell peppers, tops removed, cored, and seeded
4	green onions, trimmed and chopped
2	large tomatoes, chopped
1	tablespoon pine nuts
1	tablespoon chopped parsley
1	teaspoon freshly ground black pepper
½	teaspoon ground ginger
⅛	teaspoon cayenne pepper
3	tablespoons olive oil
½	cup plain yogurt (optional)

Preheat the oven to 400 degrees.

Place the couscous in a medium bowl. Pour the boiling water over the couscous. Cover and let stand for 10 minutes to absorb the water.

Bring a large pot of water and 1 teaspoon of the salt to a boil over high heat. Add the bell peppers. Blanch for 2 to 3 minutes. Remove the peppers from the water and place in a bowl of ice water for 10 minutes to stop the cooking process. Drain the peppers and set aside.

Combine the green onions, tomatoes, pine nuts, parsley, black pepper, ginger, cayenne pepper, and the remaining 1 teaspoon salt in a large bowl. Rake the tines of a fork across the couscous to fluff it up. Add the couscous to the tomato mixture and toss to combine.

Place the bell peppers in a large baking dish. Stuff spoonfuls of the couscous mixture inside the peppers. Drizzle the oil over the peppers. Cover with foil and bake for 15 minutes. Uncover and bake for an additional 10 minutes, or until the bell peppers are soft. Serve with a tablespoon of yogurt on top, if desired.

TANZANIAN FRIED CABBAGE

MAKES 6 SERVINGS

This simple recipe gets an extra flavor boost from the addition of the aromatic curry powder and the sweetness of the carrots.

- ¼ cup vegetable oil
- 1 small yellow onion, peeled and chopped
- 1 large tomato, sliced
- ½ teaspoon salt
- ½ teaspoon African-Style Curry Powder (page 4) or prepared curry powder
- 1 medium head cabbage
- 2 carrots, peeled and sliced into rounds
- 1 green bell pepper, seeded, ribs removed, and chopped
- ¼ cup water

Heat the oil in a large skillet over medium-high heat. Add the onion. Sauté for 2 minutes, or until soft and golden brown. Add the tomato, salt, and curry powder. Cook for 2 to 3 minutes, stirring occasionally to prevent the onion from sticking. Add the cabbage, carrots, bell pepper, and water. Reduce the heat to low, cover, and simmer for 15 to 20 minutes, or until the cabbage is crisp but tender and the liquid is absorbed.

KENYAN-STYLE MIXED GREENS

MAKES 6 SERVINGS

Coconut milk and tomatoes add remarkable flavor to this African-style "mess of greens." This recipe cherishes the nutrient-rich "pot liquor," incorporating some of the liquid from the greens in the sauce. It's delicious when served with Kenyan Polenta with Peanut Sauce *(page 36).*

1	serrano or jalapeño chile pepper, chopped (wear plastic gloves when handling)
2	teaspoons salt
2	teaspoons freshly ground black pepper
2	tablespoons olive oil
1	pound fresh collard, mustard, or turnip greens, chopped, or 1 bag (10 ounces) frozen chopped greens, thawed
1	pound fresh spinach, chopped, or 1 bag (10 ounce) frozen chopped spinach, thawed and squeezed dry
2	tablespoons butter
3	large tomatoes, cubed
1	large yellow onion, peeled and chopped
1	cup canned unsweetened coconut milk
4	teaspoons dry roasted peanuts, chopped (optional)

Fill a large pot half-full with water. Add the chile pepper, salt, black pepper, and 1 tablespoon of the olive oil. Bring to a boil over high heat. Add the greens and spinach. Reduce the heat to low and cook for 20 minutes, stirring occasionally.

Heat the remaining 1 tablespoon oil and the butter in a large skillet over medium heat. Add the tomatoes, onion, and milk and simmer for 10 minutes, stirring occasionally. Add the greens and 1 cup of the cooking liquid. Cook for 20 minutes, stirring occasionally. Taste the greens for tenderness and seasoning. Cook for an additional 10 minutes and add more seasoning, if needed. Sprinkle with the peanuts, if desired.

SOUTH AFRICAN GREEN BEANS WITH SOUR SAUCE

MAKES 6 SERVINGS

The sour-spicy sauce makes this dish a wonderfully delicious alternative to traditional American ways of preparing fresh green beans.

2	quarts water
1½	teaspoons salt
1	pound fresh green beans, trimmed
1	large egg
¼	cup malt vinegar
1	teaspoon light brown sugar
¼	teaspoon stone-ground mustard
⅛	teaspoon cayenne pepper

Bring the water and 1 teaspoon of the salt to a boil in a large pot over high heat. Drop the beans by handfuls into the boiling water and return to a boil. Reduce the heat to medium and cook the beans for 10 to 15 minutes, or until crisp but tender. Drain in a colander and place in a serving bowl.

Whisk the egg, vinegar, brown sugar, mustard, pepper, and the remaining ½ teaspoon salt together in a double boiler over medium heat. Cook for 2 to 3 minutes, whisking constantly, or until the mixture is smooth. The sauce should be slightly thick and cling to the whisk. Pour the sauce over the beans.

ETHIOPIAN *YATAKLETE KILKIL*

MAKES 8 SERVINGS

The mouth-watering mix of turmeric and chile peppers gives a spicy kick to the green beans and potatoes at the heart of this dish.

4	large white boiling potatoes, peeled and chopped
1	pound green beans, cut into 1-inch pieces, or 1 package (16 ounces) frozen green beans
2½	tablespoons olive oil
1	large yellow onion, peeled and chopped
3	cloves garlic, peeled and minced
1	small serrano chile pepper, minced, or 1 jalapeño chile pepper, minced (wear plastic gloves when handling)
1	teaspoon ground turmeric
1	teaspoon ground cumin
1	teaspoon salt
2	cans (15 ounces each) stewed tomatoes
1	teaspoon freshly squeezed lime juice
	Injera (page 48) or pita bread

Place the potatoes in a large saucepan over high heat and add just enough boiling water to cover. Cook for 12 minutes, or until tender. Add the green beans to the saucepan. Cook for 7 to 10 minutes. Drain the potatoes and beans in a colander and set aside.

Heat the oil in a large skillet over medium-high heat. Add the onion. Sauté for 7 minutes, or until slightly wilted. Add the garlic and pepper and sauté for 3 to 5 minutes. Add the turmeric, cumin, and salt and cook for 1 minute, stirring constantly. Add the tomatoes (with juice), potatoes and green beans, and the lime juice. Reduce the heat to low and cook for 10 minutes, stirring frequently, to allow the flavors to blend. Serve with Injera or pita bread.

NORTH AFRICAN-STYLE ZUCCHINI

MAKES 6 SERVINGS

The North African influence on this dish is clearly seen in the addition of almonds and raisins. The combination of ingredients produces a delectably sweet-and-sour flavor.

3	tablespoons olive oil
1	small yellow onion, peeled and thinly sliced
2	cloves garlic, peeled and crushed
1	pound zucchini, peeled and thinly sliced
¼	cup freshly squeezed lemon juice
¼	cup raisins
3	tablespoons chopped almonds
3	teaspoons light brown sugar
1	teaspoon salt
1	teaspoon freshly ground black pepper

Heat the oil in a large skillet over medium heat. Add the onion and garlic and cook for 10 minutes, stirring occasionally. Add the zucchini and stir to coat with the oil. Stir in the lemon juice, raisins, almonds, brown sugar, salt, and pepper. Reduce the heat to low and simmer for 10 to 15 minutes, stirring occasionally, or until the zucchini is tender.

MOROCCAN ZUCCHINI PANCAKES

MAKES 6 SERVINGS

The inclusion of mint in this recipe is a typical Moroccan touch. These pancakes are especially delicious when served with a spicy main dish like Senegalese Tofu (page 46).

2	large zucchini, ends trimmed
1	large yellow onion, peeled and quartered
1	large bell pepper, halved, seeded, and ribs removed
⅓	cup whole wheat or all-purpose flour
3	eggs, beaten
1	teaspoon chopped fresh mint or parsley
1	teaspoon salt
1	teaspoon freshly ground black pepper
3	tablespoons vegetable oil

Place the zucchini, onion, and bell pepper in a food processor. Pulse to mince, but do not puree. Squeeze the zucchini mixture by handfuls to remove any liquid. Pat the mixture dry with a paper towel and set aside.

Sift the flour into a large bowl. Add the eggs, mint or parsley, salt, and black pepper and stir together to make a batter. Add the zucchini mixture and stir gently to combine.

Heat the oil in a heavy skillet over medium heat until hot but not smoking. Working in batches, ladle about $\frac{1}{3}$ cup of the batter into the hot oil. Press down lightly with a spatula. Flip the pancakes when they become golden brown underneath, about 3 minutes per side.

SOUTH AFRICAN CORN PUDDING

MAKES 6 SERVINGS

This recipe is a forerunner to traditional Southern corn pudding. It is called green mealie bread in South Africa.

3	tablespoons butter, softened
3	cups fresh or frozen and thawed corn kernels
3	eggs
2	tablespoons sugar
2	tablespoons whole wheat or all-purpose flour
2	teaspoons baking powder
1	teaspoon salt
3	cups boiling water

Preheat the oven to 375 degrees. Spread 1 tablespoon of the butter on the bottom and sides of an 8-inch loaf pan.

Place the corn and eggs in a food processor or large bowl. Process or mix with an electric mixer on medium speed for 30 seconds. Add the remaining 2 tablespoons butter, the sugar, flour, baking powder, and salt. Process for another 30 seconds, or until all the ingredients are combined. Pour the mixture into the loaf pan. Cover the pan tightly with two sheets of foil, crimping the sides until the pan is thoroughly sealed.

Place the pan in a baking dish. Pour enough boiling water into the baking dish to come halfway up the sides of the loaf pan.

Bake for 1 hour, or until a toothpick inserted in the center of the pudding comes out clean. Remove the pan to a rack and cool to room temperature. Run a sharp knife around the edge of the pan and cover it with a plate. Grasp the bottom of the plate and the pan and invert them. Tap the bottom of the loaf pan. The pudding should slide out easily. Cut into slices and serve immediately.

CORN AND TOMATO CASSEROLE

MAKES 6 SERVINGS

This colorful dish is a delicious way to combine corn and tomatoes. The recipe traveled with the African captives across the waters and was often prepared in colonial households.

3	tablespoons butter, softened
2	cups fresh or frozen and thawed corn kernels
1	can (28 ounces) peeled whole tomatoes, chopped
½	cup plain soy milk
1	egg, lightly beaten
1	teaspoon light brown sugar
1½	teaspoons salt
1	teaspoon freshly ground black pepper
1	cup bread crumbs

Preheat the oven to 325 degrees. Spread 1 tablespoon of the butter on the bottom and sides of a 1½ quart baking dish.

Gently combine the corn, tomatoes (with juice), soy milk, egg, brown sugar, salt, and pepper in a large bowl. Pour the corn mixture into the baking dish. Press the mixture down with the back of a spoon until it is smooth and compact. Sprinkle the top with the bread crumbs. Place small portions of the remaining butter on top of the bread crumbs.

Bake for 30 minutes, or until the bread crumbs are golden brown and bubbles appear along the sides of the casserole.

CORN CURRY

Curry seasoning is typical in Indian recipes. A blend of African and Indian cultures is reflected in this recipe from East Africa.

1½	cups uncooked long-grain white rice
¾	cup unsweetened shredded coconut
½	cup unsalted dry roasted peanuts
1	tablespoon sesame seeds
1	teaspoon African-Style Curry Powder (page 4) or prepared curry powder
1	teaspoon salt
⅛	teaspoon cayenne pepper
2	tablespoons butter
4	cups fresh or frozen and thawed corn kernels
3	cans (14 ounces each) unsweetened coconut milk

Prepare the rice according to package directions.

Meanwhile, place the coconut, peanuts, sesame seeds, curry powder, salt, and pepper in a food processor. Process into a smooth paste.

Melt the butter in a large skillet over medium heat. Add the coconut paste. Sauté for 4 to 5 minutes, stirring constantly. Add the corn and coconut milk. Reduce the heat to low and simmer for 10 to 15 minutes, or until the ingredients thicken. Stir occasionally to prevent the mixture from sticking to the skillet. Serve over the rice.

BAKED VEGETABLE CURRY

This is a great one-dish meal that can be prepared in advance. Seasoning foods with chile pepper is a trademark of African cooking.

2	tablespoons vegetable oil
1	large yellow onion, peeled and chopped
2	cloves garlic, peeled and minced
1	serrano chile pepper, chopped (wear plastic gloves when handling)
1	teaspoon African-Style Curry Powder (page 4) or prepared curry powder
1	teaspoon salt
1	teaspoon freshly ground black pepper
3	sprigs fresh coriander leaves, chopped
5	potatoes (Yukon Gold, red, or Irish), peeled and quartered
1	pound fresh spinach, chopped, or 1 pound frozen chopped spinach, thawed and squeezed dry
½	pound cauliflower florets
1	eggplant, seeded and chopped
1	cup fresh or frozen and thawed green peas
1	can (28 ounces) peeled whole tomatoes, crushed
1	can (16 ounces) green beans, drained
1	can (15 ounces) chickpeas, rinsed and drained
1	can (14 ounces) vegetable broth

Preheat the oven to 350 degrees. Heat the oil in a large skillet over medium-high heat. Add the onion, garlic, and chile pepper and sauté until golden brown. Stir in the curry powder, salt, black pepper, and coriander.

Add the potatoes and coat them with the spices in the skillet. Cook for 2 minutes, stirring constantly.

Lightly coat a large baking dish with cooking spray. Place the potato and onion mixtures in the dish. Add the spinach, cauliflower, eggplant, peas, tomatoes (with juice), green beans, chickpeas, and vegetable broth. Stir the ingredients together to combine. Cover tightly with foil. Bake for 30 to 40 minutes, or until the potatoes are tender when pierced with a fork.

Cooking Tip: Other greens will work nicely in this recipe. Try substituting kale or collard greens for the spinach.

EGG CURRY

Hard-boiled eggs become a main dish in this spicy recipe.

1½	cups uncooked long-grain white rice
3	tablespoons butter
1	medium yellow onion, peeled and chopped
1	tablespoon whole wheat or all-purpose flour
1	teaspoon African-Style Curry Powder (page 4) or prepared curry powder
1	teaspoon salt
1	can (8 ounces) tomato sauce
½–1	cup vegetable broth
6	large eggs, hard-cooked, peeled, and halved
1	medium tomato, sliced (optional)
1	tablespoon unsalted dry roasted peanuts (optional)

Prepare the rice according to package directions.

Meanwhile, melt the butter in a large skillet over medium heat-high. Add the onions. Sauté for 7 minutes, or until golden brown. Add the flour, curry powder, and salt. Stir in the tomato sauce and ½ cup of the vegetable broth. Add more broth, if desired, for a thinner sauce. Reduce the heat to low and simmer for 10 minutes. Add the eggs and simmer for another 5 minutes. Serve over the rice and sprinkle with the tomato slices and peanuts, if desired.

GARDEN VEGETABLE COUSCOUS

This versatile recipe allows you to make full use of the beautiful bounty of vegetables available from one season to the next. Grilling various vegetables is a tasty way to prepare this dish in warmer months. Pumpkin, artichoke hearts, peas, and sweet potatoes are delicious substitutions during cooler months.

1½	cups water
4	green onions, trimmed and chopped
1	cup couscous
1	can (15 ounces) red kidney beans, rinsed and drained
2	tablespoons olive oil
2	tablespoons butter
1	small yellow onion, peeled and chopped
2	cloves garlic, peeled and minced
3	medium tomatoes, chopped
½	pound baby spinach, stems removed
1	medium bell pepper, seeded, ribs removed, and chopped
1	small zucchini, chopped
¼	pound carrots, chopped
1	teaspoon ground paprika
1	teaspoon salt
½	teaspoon ground cumin
½	teaspoon freshly ground black pepper

Bring the water and the green onions to a boil in a medium pot over high heat. Stir in the couscous and beans. Cover the pot and remove from the heat. Let the couscous stand for 10 minutes.

Meanwhile, heat the oil and butter in a medium skillet over medium-high heat. Add the onion and garlic. Sauté for 3 minutes, or until tender and golden.

Add the tomatoes, spinach, bell pepper, zucchini, carrots, paprika, salt, cumin, and black pepper to the skillet. Sauté for 10 minutes, or until the vegetables are crisp but tender.

Rake the tines of a fork across the couscous to fluff it up. Add the couscous to the vegetables and stir gently to combine.

CONCOMBRE EN DAUBE WITH MASHED VEGETABLES

MAKES 6 SERVINGS

Concombre en Daube, *or stewed cucumbers, is especially delicious with mashed vegetables, a common side dish in most parts of Africa. Other vegetables that are used in the African version of this recipe are cassava or yucca tubers, taro, and coco yams.*

CONCOMBRE EN DAUBE

- 3 tablespoons olive oil or vegetable oil
- 1 medium yellow onion, peeled and chopped
- 1 can (20 ounces) peeled whole tomatoes
- 3 medium cucumbers, peeled, halved, seeded, and thickly sliced
- 1 teaspoon salt
- 1 teaspoon freshly ground black pepper
- ¼ teaspoon sugar

MASHED VEGETABLES

- 2 green plantains, peeled and quartered
- 4 red potatoes, scrubbed
- 2 sweet potatoes, peeled and quartered
- 2 teaspoons salt
- ⅛ teaspoon cayenne pepper
- 2 tablespoons olive oil

To prepare the *Concombre en Daube*: Heat the oil in a medium saucepan over medium-high heat. Add the onion. Sauté for 10 minutes, or until golden and tender. Add the tomatoes (with juice), cucumbers, salt, pepper, and sugar. Reduce the heat to low, cover, and simmer for 20 to 30 minutes.

To prepare the mashed vegetables: Meanwhile fill a large pot with 6 cups water. Add the plantains, red potatoes, sweet potatoes, and 1 teaspoon of the salt. Cover and boil over high heat for 20 minutes, or until the sweet potatoes are tender. Drain most of the water from the pan, leaving about ½ cup in the pot to moisten the vegetables. Add the pepper, oil, and the remaining 1 teaspoon salt. Mash with a potato masher or an immersion blender until smooth. Serve topped with the *Concombre en Daube*.

CONGO MOAMBE

There are many variations of this dish. Here I've created a vegetarian version that includes eggplant, a common ingredient in certain parts of the African continent. I love combining olive oil with butter. The oil keeps the butter from burning, and the butter adds flavor to the oil and the ingredients. This sauce is also delicious served over couscous. Or, try it over Kenyan Vermicelli Bread (page 51).

1½	cups uncooked long-grain white rice
2	tablespoons olive oil
2	tablespoons butter
1	yellow onion, peeled and finely chopped
1½	pounds eggplant, peeled and cut into ½-inch cubes
2	cloves garlic, peeled and minced
2½	cups tomato sauce
1	teaspoon salt
1	teaspoon cayenne pepper
1	teaspoon sugar
½	teaspoon freshly grated nutmeg
½	cup smooth peanut butter

Prepare the rice according to package directions.

Meanwhile, heat the oil in a large saucepan over medium-high heat. Add the butter and stir until melted. Add the onion. Sauté for 7 minutes, or until wilted. Add the eggplant and garlic. Reduce the heat to low and sauté for 10 minutes, or until the eggplant is golden and soft. Add the tomato sauce, salt, pepper, sugar, and nutmeg and simmer for 5 minutes. Taste the sauce and add more salt, if needed.

Remove 1 cup of the tomato sauce mixture from the saucepan and place in a medium bowl. Microwave the peanut butter in a small bowl for 30 seconds, or until soft. Stir into the bowl with the tomato sauce mixture until smooth and slightly liquefied. Add the peanut butter mixture to the saucepan to thicken the sauce. Simmer for another 10 minutes to blend the flavors. Serve over the rice.

EAST AFRICAN FRIED OKRA

MAKES 4 TO 6 SERVINGS

Okra is an African plant that traveled across the waters and became a staple ingredient in the cuisine of the American South.

3	tablespoons freshly squeezed lemon juice
1	tablespoon garlic powder
2	teaspoons African-Style Curry Powder (page 4) or prepared curry powder
1	teaspoon freshly ground black pepper
12	small to medium okra pods, tips removed but stems left intact
1	cup vegetable oil
1	teaspoon salt

Combine the lemon juice, garlic powder, turmeric, curry powder, and pepper in a small bowl.

Cut the okra lengthwise, leaving the stem end intact so that the 2 halves remain connected. Smooth the spice mixture inside and outside the okra. Press the sides together firmly.

Heat the oil in a large skillet over medium-high heat until hot but not smoking. Fry the okra for 3 to 4 minutes, or until lightly browned. Remove to a paper towel–covered plate to drain. Sprinkle with the salt.

Cooking Tip: Choose green or red okra pods that are 2 to 3 inches long to ensure that the okra will be tender. Bigger okra pods are often tough. Adding lemon juice removes the slippery texture in okra that many people find distasteful.

CHICKPEA CROQUETTES

MAKES 6 SERVINGS

These protein-packed croquettes are great for days when you want to fix something straight from the pantry for a quick dinner. They're delicious topped with Veggie Gravy (page 176). Or serve with Cucumber and Pepper Relish (page 5).

2	cans (15 ounces each) chickpeas, rinsed and drained
2	cloves garlic, peeled and crushed
1	bunch green onions, trimmed and chopped
2	teaspoons ground cumin
2	teaspoons ground coriander
2	tablespoons chopped fresh cilantro
1	small egg, beaten
2	tablespoons whole wheat or all-purpose flour
1	teaspoon salt
1	teaspoon freshly ground black pepper
1/8	teaspoon cayenne pepper
1/4	cup vegetable oil

Place the chickpeas in a food processor and process until smooth. Add the garlic, green onions, cumin, and coriander. Process until well-combined. Scrape the chickpea mixture into a medium bowl. Add the cilantro, egg, flour, salt, black pepper, and cayenne pepper. Stir well, adding more flour if necessary to form the mixture into a dough.

Dust your hands with flour to prevent the dough from sticking to your fingers. Shape the dough into 12 patties. Place on a plate, cover with plastic wrap, and refrigerate for 30 minutes.

Heat the oil in a large skillet over medium-high heat until hot but not smoking. Fry the patties for 2 to 3 minutes on each side, or until crisp and golden brown. Remove from the oil to a paper towel–covered plate to drain.

KENYAN POLENTA WITH PEANUT SAUCE

MAKES 6 SERVINGS

This polenta dish is called Ugali *in Kenya. The grits used here are white hominy that's been dried and then coarsely ground. The Ghanaian word for dried white hominy is* kinke. *We call it grits in the South and polenta when we're in high-priced restaurants. Through the years, grits have moved from dinner to breakfast and back again, with delicious results.*

SAUCE

- 2 tablespoons olive oil
- 1 medium yellow onion, peeled and chopped
- 3 cloves garlic, peeled and minced
- 2 medium tomatoes, chopped
- 1 medium green bell pepper, seeded, ribs removed, and chopped
- 1 jalapeño chile pepper, seeded and chopped (wear plastic gloves when handling)
- 1 teaspoon salt
- 1 teaspoon freshly ground black pepper
- ⅛ teaspoon cayenne pepper
- 1 small eggplant, chopped
- ½ cup smooth peanut butter
- ¼ cup hot water (120 to 130 degrees)

POLENTA

- 4 cups vegetable broth
- 2 cups hominy grits (not quick-cooking)
- 2 tablespoons butter
- 1 teaspoon salt

To prepare the sauce: Heat the oil in a large skillet over medium-high heat. Add the onion and garlic. Sauté for 7 minutes, or until the onion is golden. Add the tomatoes, bell pepper, chile pepper, salt, black pepper, and cayenne pepper and cook for 10 minutes. Add the eggplant and cook for an additional 5 minutes.

Combine the peanut butter and the hot water in a small bowl. Stir until the peanut butter forms a smooth paste. Add to the pan with the eggplant mixture. Reduce the heat to low and simmer for 10 minutes, stirring occasionally, or until the eggplant is tender.

To prepare the polenta: Bring the vegetable broth to a boil in a large saucepan over medium heat. Slowly stir in the grits. Continue to cook for 5 to 7 minutes, stirring constantly, or until the polenta reaches a thick consistency. Stir in the butter and salt.

Place the polenta in individual serving bowls topped with several heaping tablespoons of the peanut sauce.

KOSHERI

Kosheri (*also spelled* kosheree, kochary, kushari, *and* kochari) *is the only menu item sold in some specialty restaurants in Egypt. As the saying goes, you can have anything you want to eat, as long as it's* kosheri *in a small, medium, or large serving! Kosheri is also a popular street-vendor dish.*

1½	cups uncooked long-grain white rice
½	cup vegetable oil
1	cup whole wheat or all-purpose flour
3	teaspoons salt
2	teaspoons freshly ground black pepper
¼	teaspoon cayenne pepper
2	large yellow onions, peeled and cut into rings
2	cloves garlic, peeled and minced
1	jalapeño chile pepper, seeded and chopped (wear plastic gloves when handling)
2	cans (20 ounces each) peeled whole tomatoes, crushed
1	can (15 ounces) lentils, rinsed and drained
1	cup vegetable broth
¼	cup white wine vinegar
½	teaspoon ground cumin

Prepare the rice according to the package directions.

Meanwhile, heat the oil in a large skillet over medium-high heat until hot but not smoking.

Combine the flour, 1 teaspoon of the salt, 1 teaspoon of the black pepper, and 1/8 teaspoon of the cayenne pepper in a shallow bowl. Dredge the onion rings in the seasoned flour. Place the onions in the hot oil and fry for 3 to 4 minutes. Turn the onions over and fry until golden brown on both sides. Remove from the oil to a paper towel–covered plate to drain. (Do not discard the oil in the pan.) Sprinkle the onions with 1 teaspoon of the remaining salt. Set aside.

Place the garlic and the chile pepper in the remaining vegetable oil in the skillet. Sauté for 3 minutes. Add the tomatoes (with juice), lentils, vegetable broth, vinegar, cumin, and the remaining 1 teaspoon salt, 1 teaspoon black pepper, and 1/8 teaspoon cayenne pepper to the skillet. Reduce the heat to low and simmer for 8 to 10 minutes.

Place a thin layer of the sauce on the bottom of a large serving dish. Place the rice on top of the sauce. Top with a layer of the onions. Place another layer of the sauce on top of the onions. Continue layering until all the ingredients have been used. Top with any remaining sauce and fried onions.

Cooking Tip: When I'm in a rush, I've made this recipe in record time by using canned fried onions and reheated leftover cooked rice.

DJAJA TARAT (THE CHICKEN THAT FLEW)

I don't know how this Moroccan dish got its name. I would imagine that it normally includes chicken, an ingredient that would be excluded during some religious holidays. It still has enough protein to be a main-course dish, even without the chicken in the pot!

3	tablespoons olive oil
1	medium yellow onion, peeled and sliced
1	can (15 ounces) chickpeas, rinsed and drained
2	large sweet potatoes, peeled and cubed
¾	cup finely chopped fresh cilantro, stems discarded
1	teaspoon salt
1	teaspoon freshly ground black pepper
⅛	teaspoon saffron filaments
½	cup plain soy milk

Heat the oil in a large saucepan over medium-high heat. Add the onion. Sauté for 7 to 10 minutes, or until soft and golden. Add the chickpeas, sweet potatoes, cilantro, salt, pepper, saffron, and soy milk. Reduce the heat to low and simmer for 15 to 20 minutes.

SOUTH AFRICAN SAMP AND COWPEAS
(SOUTH AFRICAN *UMNGQUSHO*)

MAKES 6 SERVINGS

Nelson Mandela referred to this dish in his book Long Walk to Freedom. *Samp, or mealies, is the name for dried corn, or hominy, in many African dialects. Cowpeas are what Americans refer to as black-eyed peas. Mandela recalls how the women prepared samp and cowpeas: "When preparing the mealies, the women used different methods. They could ground the kernels between two stones to make bread, or boil the mealies first, producing* umphothulo *(mealie flour eaten with sour milk) or um-ngqusho (samp, sometimes plain or mixed with beans). Unlike mealies, which were sometimes in short supply, milk from our cows and goats was always plentiful." This is an easier version of the South African recipe.*

1	tablespoon butter
1	tablespoon peanut oil or vegetable oil
1	medium yellow onion, peeled and chopped
1	can (15 ounces) hominy, with the liquid and lightly mashed
1	can (15 ounces) black-eyed peas, with liquid
1	teaspoon salt
1	teaspoon freshly ground black pepper
⅛	teaspoon cayenne pepper
½	teaspoon freshly squeezed lemon juice

Heat the butter and the oil in a medium pot over medium heat. Add the onion and cook for 3 minutes, until tender. Add the hominy, peas, salt, black pepper, and cayenne pepper. Cook for 8 to 10 minutes to blend the flavors, stirring occasionally. Stir in the lemon juice.

MOROCCAN POTATO CASSEROLE

MAKES 8 SERVINGS

This aromatic one-pot meal is a sensory ticket to Morocco.

6	cloves garlic, peeled
2	teaspoons salt
2	teaspoons ground paprika
½	teaspoon ground cumin
¼	teaspoon cayenne pepper
¾	cup chopped fresh cilantro
¾	cup chopped parsley
6	tablespoons olive oil
3	tablespoons red wine vinegar
2	tablespoons freshly squeezed lemon juice
1½	pounds red potatoes, scrubbed and sliced ½-inch thick
4	ribs celery, cut into 2-inch pieces
3	large red or green bell peppers, seeded, ribs removed, and cut into strips
4	large tomatoes, cut into eighths

Place the garlic, ½ teaspoon of the salt, the paprika, cumin, and cayenne pepper in a food processor or blender. Process to form a paste. Add the cilantro and parsley and pulse a few times. Add 3 tablespoons of the oil, the vinegar, lemon juice, and ½ teaspoon of the remaining salt. Blend well.

Combine the potatoes, celery, bell peppers, and the remaining 1 teaspoon salt in a large bowl. Add the sauce to the bowl and toss to coat the vegetables. Spread the potato mixture in an even layer in a large, shallow baking dish. Scatter the tomatoes over the top. Drizzle the remaining 3 tablespoons oil over top of the tomatoes.

Tightly cover the pan with foil. Bake for 35 minutes. Remove the foil and bake for another 20 to 30 minutes, or until the vegetables are tender.

YELLOW RICE

Turmeric is the spice that gives curry powder its yellow color and rich aroma. It is a common seasoning in India and is often used in Northern African cooking.

2	tablespoons olive oil
2	tablespoons butter
2	cups uncooked long-grain white rice
3½	cups water
2	sticks cinnamon
1	teaspoon salt
1	teaspoon ground turmeric
1	cup raisins (optional)

Heat the oil and butter in a large skillet over medium heat until the butter is melted. Add the rice. Stir to coat the rice with the oil. Add the water, cinnamon sticks, salt, and turmeric. Bring to a boil over high heat. Reduce the heat to low, cover, and simmer for 15 to 20 minutes, or until the rice is tender and all the liquid is absorbed. Stir in the raisins, if desired. Remove and discard the cinnamon sticks before serving.

SIERRA LEONE *JOLLOF* RICE

MAKES 8 SERVINGS

This is a spicy vegetarian version of the popular West African dish also known as Wolof rice. It is the forerunner of jambalaya, the popular Creole dish that combines fish, sausage, and poultry.

3	tablespoons olive oil
2	medium yellow onions, peeled and chopped
4	cloves garlic, peeled and minced
1	large red or green bell pepper, seeded, ribs removed, and chopped
1	jalapeño chile pepper, seeds and stems removed, chopped (wear plastic gloves when handling)
1	cup uncooked long-grain white rice
1	teaspoon salt
1	teaspoon ground ginger
½	teaspoon African-Style Curry Powder (page 4) or prepared curry powder
¼	teaspoon cayenne pepper
2½	cups vegetable broth
2	large tomatoes, chopped
2	tablespoons tomato paste
2	bay leaves
2	pounds eggplant, cubed
1	can (16 ounces) black-eyed peas, drained
½	pound fresh green beans, trimmed and cut into 1-inch pieces, or ½ pound frozen and thawed green beans

Heat the oil in a large skillet over medium-high heat. Add the onions, garlic, bell pepper, and chile pepper. Sauté for 3 to 5 minutes, or until the onion is tender. Add the rice, salt, ginger, curry powder, and cayenne pepper. Stir to coat the rice with the oil and seasonings. Add the vegetable broth, tomatoes, tomato paste, and bay leaves. Bring to a boil over high heat. Add the eggplant, black-eyed peas, and green beans. Reduce the heat to low, cover, and simmer for 20 to 30 minutes, or until the rice is tender and the liquid absorbed. Remove and discard the bay leaves before serving.

NORTH AFRICAN BULGUR AND VERMICELLI PILAF

MAKES 6 SERVINGS

The addition of fried onions and bulgur wheat provides an unusual and flavorful change from traditional pilaf recipes.

1	cup canned fried onions
1¼	cups bulgur wheat
2	tablespoons olive oil
1	medium yellow onion, peeled and sliced
1	green bell pepper, seeded, ribs removed, and sliced
1	ounce vermicelli, broken into pieces
1½	cups vegetable broth
2	large tomatoes, chopped
1	teaspoon salt
1	teaspoon freshly ground black pepper
2	tablespoons chopped parsley

Preheat the oven to 400 degrees.

Spread the fried onions on a baking sheet. Crisp the onions for 3 to 5 minutes in the oven. Set aside and keep warm.

Place the bulgur wheat in a colander and rinse with cold water. Drain the bulgur wheat and set aside.

Heat the oil in a large saucepan over medium-high heat. Add the yellow onion and bell pepper. Sauté for 5 minutes, or until the onion is golden and soft. Add the vermicelli and stir to coat with the oil. Add the bulgur wheat to the pan. Pour in the vegetable broth and bring to a boil. Reduce the heat to low, cover, and simmer for 5 minutes. Add the tomatoes, salt, and black pepper. Cook for an additional 8 to 10 minutes, or until the bulgur wheat is tender and the stock is absorbed.

Place the pilaf in a serving bowl and stir in the parsley. Sprinkle the fried onions over the pilaf.

SENEGALASE TOFU

MAKES 4 SERVINGS

This spicy dish reflects a blend of cultures from Africa to Asia.

3	tablespoons vegetable oil
½	cup chunky peanut butter
¼	cup freshly squeezed lemon juice
1	large yellow onion, peeled and chopped
1	serrano chile pepper, minced (wear plastic gloves when handling)
2	cloves garlic, peeled and minced
2	springs fresh thyme, finely chopped
1	teaspoon salt
1	teaspoon freshly ground black pepper
1	pound firm, silken tofu, drained and cut into ½-inch slices

Combine the vegetable oil, peanut butter, lemon juice, onion, chile pepper, garlic, thyme, salt, and black pepper in a baking dish. Place the tofu slices in the peanut butter mixture and stir to coat. Marinate the tofu at room temperature for at least 30 minutes.

Preheat the broiler.

Broil the tofu for 3 to 5 minutes, or until lightly browned. Turn the tofu and brown the bottom for 2 minutes.

PEANUT BISCUITS

In Africa, tasty biscuits are often eaten as a snack called kulikuli *(pronounced cooli-cooli). This is a wonderfully protein-rich Ethnic Vegetarian version of the African treat. The biscuits are perfect to pair with a salad.*

⅔ cup vanilla-flavored soy milk
½ cup smooth peanut butter
2 tablespoons brown sugar
1¾ cups biscuit mix
¼ cup vegetable protein flakes (soy flakes)
   Whole wheat or all-purpose flour

Preheat the oven to 450 degrees.

Place the soy milk, peanut butter, and brown sugar in a food processor or blender. Process on high speed until smooth and well-blended. Add the biscuit mix and protein flakes and process to form a dough.

Lightly flour a cutting board. Scrape out the dough onto the board. Knead gently a few times. Pat the dough out into a rectangle about ¾ inches in thickness. Dip a biscuit cutter or the rim of a small drinking glass into some flour. Cut the dough into 2-inch rounds. Bake on an ungreased baking sheet for 11 to 13 minutes, or until lightly browned.

ETHIOPIAN FLAT BREAD (INJERA)

Injera *is a must for most Ethiopian meals. The entire evening's meal is served on this pancake-like bread; it's also used as the plate and the eating utensil. Everyone at the table eats from the same serving dish. The proper way to eat a meal served on* injera *is to use two fingers and the thumb of your right hand to wrap up a small portion of food in the bread, then pop it into your mouth.* Injera *is traditionally made from teff, a highly nutritious cereal grain similar to rye. Teff is ground into a flour and mixed with water to make the fermented batterlike dough used for* injera. *This is an easier version of the authentic recipe. It takes some practice to get it perfect, but don't get discouraged—it is well worth the effort!*

- 4 cups self-rising flour
- 1 cup whole wheat flour
- 1 teaspoon baking powder
- 3 cups water
- 2 cups club soda

Combine the self-rising flour, whole wheat flour, and baking powder in a large bowl. Slowly add the water and club soda, mixing until the batter is smooth and pours off the mixing spoon in a thin stream. Add more water if the batter is too thick.

Heat a large nonstick skillet over medium heat until a drop of water bounces on the surface of the pan. Quickly ladle the batter into the pan until it covers the bottom. Remove the pan from the heat and swirl it around gently to allow the batter to evenly coat the bottom. Return to the heat. Cook for 2 to 3 minutes, or until small holes appear on the surface. Remove with a spatula immediately. (Injera is only cooked on one side.) They should be light in color, slightly spongy in texture, and pliable, similar to a French crepe. The injera should not be crispy or brown.

Stack the injera in layers as you cook them, covering with a clean cloth to prevent them from drying out. Serve on a platter, placing them in an overlapping concentric circle, beginning with the inside and overlapping each piece to the outer edges of the platter.

FU FU

Fu fu *is a common side dish in many parts of West Africa. It is usually served with soups and stews. My African friends often take a pinch of* fu fu, *dip it into their soup or stew, and then pop it into their mouths! This is an easier version of the traditional recipe, which sometimes requires two people to prepare (one person holds the pot while the other stirs the thick mixture vigorously until it forms a ball). Adding the protein flakes increases the nutritional value of the dish.*

4	cups water
1¼	cups cream of wheat (not instant)
¾	cup potato flakes
¼	cup vegetable protein flakes (soy flakes)
1	tablespoon butter
⅛	teaspoon salt

Bring 2 cups of the water to boil in a small saucepan over medium heat. Reduce the heat to low.

Bring the remaining 2 cups of water to a boil in a large saucepan over high heat. Reduce the heat to medium. Add ¼ cup of the cream of wheat to the water, stirring constantly. Stir in the remaining 1 cup cream of wheat, ¼ cup at a time, the potato flakes, and protein flakes until the mixture is thick but smooth. If the mixture is too thick, add the hot water from the small saucepan, a few tablespoons at a time, to make it easier to stir. Add the butter and salt, stirring until the butter melts. Continue to cook and stir the mixture for 6 to 8 minutes, or until the fu fu pulls away from the sides of the pan and forms a ball. Scoop the fu fu into fist-size balls and place them in individual serving bowls.

LIBERIAN PINEAPPLE NUT BREAD

MAKES 2 LOAVES

Eighty-six African captives traveled from America to Liberia, West Africa, in 1820 to escape slavery and form a free Black colony there. The citizens of Liberia overcame many hardships to emerge as a proud—and free—republic in 1847. I've found that recipes from Liberia are a unique blend of African and African-American culinary traditions. This pineapple bread is easy to make and tastes even better the second day.

3	large eggs, beaten
2	cups crushed pineapple, with juice
1	cup pineapple juice
5	cups whole wheat or all-purpose flour
1½	cups wheat bran
2	tablespoons baking powder
2	teaspoons baking soda
2	teaspoons salt
1	cup roasted peanuts, finely chopped

Preheat the oven to 350 degrees. Grease the bottom only of two 9 × 5 × 3-inch loaf pans.

Combine the eggs, the pineapple, and pineapple juice in a large bowl. Sift the flour, wheat bran, baking powder, baking soda, and salt together in a medium bowl. Add the flour mixture to the egg mixture, 1 cup at a time, stirring until the ingredients are well-combined and form a soft dough. Add the peanuts, mixing well. Divide the dough evenly between the prepared loaf pans.

Bake for 1 hour, or until a toothpick inserted in the center of the loaves comes out clean. Cool slightly. Run a sharp knife around the edge of the pan to loosen the sides of the loaves from the pans. Remove the loaves from the pans. Cool completely before slicing.

To store, wrap well and refrigerate. The loaves should keep for at least a week.

KENYAN VERMICELLI BREAD

MAKES 12 SERVINGS

This moist "bread" makes a flavorful accompaniment when topped by a serving of Concombre en Daube *(page 32) or* Baked Vegetable Curry *(page 29). Or try serving it with* Congo Moambe *sauce (page 33).*

½	pound vermicelli
4	cups unsweetened coconut milk
½	cup sugar
¼	teaspoon ground ginger
1	egg
½	cup whole wheat or all-purpose flour

Preheat the oven to 350 degrees. Coat a 13 × 9-inch baking dish with cooking spray.

Prepare the vermicelli according to package directions. Drain in a colander.

Heat the coconut milk and sugar in a large saucepan over medium heat. Bring the mixture to a boil, stirring constantly. Reduce the heat to low and cook for 5 minutes. Add the vermicelli and ginger.

Beat the egg in a small bowl. Add 1 or 2 tablespoons of the coconut milk mixture to the beaten egg, then stir the egg mixture into the pan. Whisk in the flour. Pour the mixture into the prepared baking dish

Bake for 1 hour, or until soft and spongy. Cut into squares to serve.

PERI-PERI MUFFINS

MAKES 12 LARGE MUFFINS

These spicy muffins are popular in West Africa. They are traditionally seasoned with the peri-peri chile pepper. I've made a few substitutions and added cayenne pepper because it is easier to find in America. The muffins may have an American accent now, but they've retained their fiery African flavor.

½	cup butter
¼	cup sugar
1	teaspoon cayenne pepper
½	teaspoon salt
2	eggs, lightly beaten
½	cup plain soy milk
1½	cups whole wheat or all-purpose flour
1	teaspoon baking powder
¾	cup finely chopped unsalted peanuts
½	cup honey

Preheat the oven to 400 degrees. Lightly grease a 12-cup muffin tin.

Combine the butter, sugar, cayenne pepper, and salt in a large bowl until the mixture is creamy and light. Stir in the eggs and soy milk until the batter is well-blended.

Sift the flour and baking powder into a medium bowl. Add the flour mixture to the batter, $\frac{1}{2}$ cup at a time, stirring until the batter is smooth. Stir in $\frac{1}{2}$ cup of the peanuts. Spoon the batter into the prepared muffin cups until the cups are about one-third full. Sprinkle the remaining peanuts on top.

Bake for 12 minutes. Run a sharp knife around the edge of each muffin to loosen them from the cups. Remove the muffins from the pan. Microwave the honey for 20 seconds, or until warm. Drizzle the honey over the tops of the warm muffins.

WEST AFRICAN FRUIT FRITTERS

This recipe makes a beautiful presentation and puts the "orphaned" contents of your fruit bowl to good use.

1	egg, separated
⅓	cup water
2	teaspoons vegetable oil
1	teaspoon freshly squeezed lemon juice or lime juice
½	cup whole wheat or all-purpose flour
1	tablespoon granulated sugar
⅛	teaspoon salt
¼	teaspoon cream of tartar
	Vegetable oil for frying
2	small bananas, sliced
1	large orange, peeled and divided into segments
1	cup cubed pineapple
1	cup cubed papaya
½	cup confectioners' sugar (optional)
	Lime or lemon wedges

Place the egg yolk and water in a large bowl. Clean the beaters of the electric mixer thoroughly so the egg whites will stiffen properly. With an electric mixer on medium speed, beat briefly to combine. Add the 2 teaspoons oil, lemon juice or lime juice, flour, granulated sugar, and salt. Beat until the batter is smooth and well-combined.

Place the egg white and cream of tartar in a small glass bowl. With the electric mixer on high speed, beat until stiff peaks form. Gently fold the egg whites into the batter.

Heat the oil in a large skillet over high heat. Using tongs, dip the banana, orange, pineapple, and papaya pieces into the batter. Shake off the excess batter and place the fruit in the hot oil. Cook for 3 to 4 minutes, or until the batter turns a golden brown. Remove the fruit from the oil to a paper towel–covered plate to drain. Sprinkle the fruit with the confectioners' sugar, if desired. Serve with lime or lemon wedges.

TANZANIAN BAKED BANANAS

MAKES 4 SERVINGS

This is like an African version of Bananas Foster. It's so simple that you can let it bake during dinner and then serve it for dessert.

4	large, ripe, unpeeled bananas
¼	cup butter, melted
½	cup packed brown sugar
1	tablespoon freshly squeezed lemon juice

Preheat the oven to 425 degrees.

Cut off the ends of the bananas, but do not peel them. Place the bananas on an ungreased baking sheet or in a baking pan. Bake for 15 minutes, or until the skins burst and turn black. Cut the bananas lengthwise and peel off and discard the skins. Place in a serving bowl.

Combine the butter, brown sugar, and lemon juice in a small bowl. Drizzle the brown sugar mixture over the bananas.

MOROCCAN ALMOND MILK

This is a wonderful drink to serve after dinner or before bedtime. If you want to use honey-roasted almonds, you can decrease the amount of brown sugar by half. I've replaced cow's milk with soy milk to make it even more soothing and nutritious.

1½   cups roasted almonds
½   cup packed brown sugar
1   cup water
2   cups vanilla-flavored soy milk
1   tablespoon orange zest

Place the almonds and brown sugar in a food processor and process into a powder. Add ½ cup of the water and process until smooth. Let the mixture rest for 30 minutes.

With the motor running, slowly add the remaining ½ cup water and process until smooth. Let the mixture rest for an additional 30 minutes.

Warm the soy milk in a medium saucepan over low heat. Do not boil the soy milk. Stir in the orange zest and almond mixture. Stir well and serve immediately.

SPICED RICE DRINK

In Lagos and other parts of Nigeria, this aromatic drink is served for breakfast or as a dessert. Using soy milk adds nutritional benefit to this treat.

2	tablespoons uncooked long-grain white rice
1	quart vanilla-flavored soy milk
2	teaspoons sugar
¼	teaspoon ground cinnamon
¼	teaspoon freshly grated nutmeg
¼	teaspoon lemon zest

Place the rice and milk in a medium saucepan and bring to a boil over medium heat. Reduce the heat to low and simmer for 30 minutes, stirring occasionally. Strain the mixture over a bowl through a fine sieve or a piece of cheesecloth to remove the rice. Stir in the sugar, cinnamon, nutmeg, and lemon zest. Chill in the refrigerator then serve.

LEMON GRASS TEA

MAKES 4 SERVINGS

Lemon grass is a common ingredient in Asian and Caribbean cuisine. The herb is often prepared as a tea that is consumed hot or cold for medicinal purposes—it is said to aid in digestion and assist with the relief of muscle cramps and headaches. The bulb is pounded and bruised to release its flavor and then the entire stalk of grass is minced and added to recipes. In my garden, this fragrant herb grows so rapidly an abundantly that it truly lives up to its name.

1   bundle (2½ to 3 ounces) lemon grass
1   quart water
1   cup sugar

Wash the lemon grass, and place it in a large pot. Add 2 cups of the water. Cover and simmer gently over medium heat for 5 to 8 minutes. Remove the pot from the heat. Cool slightly and strain the liquid into a pitcher. Stir in the sugar and the remaining 2 cups water. Serve the tea warm or chill to serve cold.

AFRO-CARIBBEAN VEGETARIAN RECIPES

IN ACCEPTING A WEDDING INVITATION FROM friends, my husband, Michael, and I finally found ourselves on the Caribbean vacation of our dreams. The entire wedding party traveled together on a cruise to the Grand Cayman Islands. It was our first exposure to a tropical lifestyle, and we loved everything about it, especially the food!

During our stops at various ports, we couldn't get enough of these bright, refreshing flavors. I wanted to bring it all home with me, so I purchased jerk seasonings, Jamaican marmalades flavored with bitter Seville oranges, hot sauces made from fresh, local ingredients, and cookbooks so I could relive a little bit of our first cruise through my home-cooking.

The origins of Afro-Caribbean cuisine date back to the time when African captives were brought to the region to labor in the homes and fields of vast sugarcane plantations owned by Europeans. Slave cooks adapted the culinary knowledge and a few staples that arrived with them from their African homelands to the ingredients and methods they found on the islands. The resulting blend of African, Amerindian, and European cooking gave rise to Afro-Caribbean cuisine.

The slaves cultivated okra, yams, and various types of beans and greens and prepared them in much the same way they had in Africa. The evolution of some dishes is easy to see—for example, African *fufu* (page 49) became *coo coo* (page 79) in the Caribbean, where it is made out of cornmeal. But for the most part, African culinary influence throughout the islands is difficult to trace in detail. Still, there is certainly no question that African culinary influence permeates the entire region—island cooks still use various African methods and types of cooking vessels, including three-legged pots called spiders and utensils called calabashes, which are made from gourds.

Afro-Caribbean cooking has ingenious ways with fresh ingredients and peppery spices. The flavors may be unfamiliar to you, but as an old island proverb says, "The looks ah de pudding is not de taste." Try something new!

59

■ CONDIMENTS AND SALADS ■

■ SOUPS AND STEWS ■

■ MAIN DISHES ■

■ BREADS AND DESSERTS ■

■ BEVERAGES ■

JERK SEASONING

MAKES 1 CUP

Jerk is the Caribbean name for the distinctive blend of spices that were created by the Arawak Indians, the Islands' first settlers. A group of Africans called the Maroons escaped from various plantations in Jamaica and used the jerk method of preserving meat to survive while evading their captors. They used guerilla tactics to fight against their slaveholders. Eventually they won their freedom.

4	cloves garlic, peeled
4	sprigs fresh thyme or 1 tablespoon dried
3	bay leaves
3	green onions, trimmed
1	jalapeño chile pepper, stem removed (wear plastic gloves when handling)
1½	teaspoons onion powder
1	teaspoon salt
1	teaspoon freshly ground black pepper
1	tablespoon ground allspice
½	teaspoon dried oregano leaves
½	teaspoon ground ginger
½	teaspoon ground paprika
½	teaspoon freshly grated nutmeg
¼	teaspoon cayenne pepper

Place the garlic, thyme, bay leaves, green onions, and chile pepper in a food processor. Process to chop finely. Add the onion powder, salt, black pepper, allspice, oregano, ginger, paprika, nutmeg, and cayenne pepper. Process to grind for 1 minute. Place the jerk seasoning in an airtight container in a cool, dry place.

MANGO CHUTNEY

MAKES 8 CUPS

My librarian friend, Jeanette Larson, was one of the first people to introduce me to the vegetarian lifestyle and this fabulous chutney recipe.

8	firm, ripe mangos, peeled and sliced
3	cups packed brown sugar
2½	cups cider vinegar
2	cups raisins
1	large green bell pepper, seeded, ribs removed, and chopped
1	small yellow onion, peeled and chopped
1	piece (1 inch) ginger root, peeled and finely chopped
1	jalapeño chile pepper, chopped (wear plastic gloves when handling)
1	teaspoon freshly ground black pepper
1	teaspoon salt

Place all ingredients in a large, noncorrosive saucepan. Bring to a boil over high heat, stirring to combine the ingredients. Reduce the heat to low and simmer for 30 minutes, or until the mixture is thick. Cool for 15 minutes. Stir vigorously, place in an airtight container, and refrigerate.

ISLAND SALSA

MAKES 6 CUPS

This salsa provides a flavorful burst of protein when used as a condiment for vegetarian dishes.

1   tablespoon olive oil
2   cloves garlic, peeled and minced
1   medium yellow onion, peeled and chopped
1   medium green bell pepper, seeded, ribs removed, and chopped
1   can (15 ounces) black beans, rinsed and drained
1   can (15 ounces) whole kernel corn, drained
1   can (15 ounces) stewed tomatoes
1   papaya, peeled and sliced
1   teaspoon ground cumin
1   teaspoon freshly ground black pepper
1   teaspoon salt
½   teaspoon sugar
2   tablespoons chopped fresh cilantro

Heat the oil in a large saucepan over medium-high heat. Add the garlic, onion, and bell pepper. Sauté for 5 to 10 minutes, or until the vegetables are soft. Add the beans, corn, tomatoes (with juice), papaya, cumin, black pepper, salt, and sugar. Stir to combine. Reduce the heat to low and simmer for 5 to 10 minutes, stirring frequently. Stir in the cilantro. Remove from the heat. Store in an airtight container and refrigerate.

TOMATILLO DRESSING

MAKES ABOUT 2½ CUPS

Tomatillos, a familiar ingredient in Caribbean recipes, are grown throughout the Spanish-speaking islands. They are, like tomatoes, members of the nightshade family, and they add a distinctive texture and flavor to any sauce. Tomatillos have a sour taste, but smaller ones are sweeter. The inedible papery husks need to be removed before cooking.

3	green tomatillos, husks removed and chopped
⅓	cup pine nuts, toasted
6	sprigs parsley, chopped
6	sprigs fresh cilantro, chopped
3	cloves garlic, peeled
2	hard-cooked egg yolks
2	tablespoons capers, drained
1	teaspoon dry mustard
1	teaspoon salt
1	teaspoon freshly ground black pepper
¾	cup olive oil
	Juice of 1 large lime

Place the tomatillos, pine nuts, parsley, cilantro, garlic, egg yolks, capers, mustard, salt, and pepper in a food processor. Process to puree. With the motor running, slowly add the oil until the ingredients are emulsified and the sauce thickens to the consistency of mayonnaise. Add the lime juice and pulse to combine. Store the sauce in an airtight container and refrigerate.

RASTA RICE SALAD

MAKES 4 SERVINGS; 1 CUP DRESSING

Rastafarian culture and religion are part of life in much of the Caribbean. Many Rastafarians are vegetarians. This island favorite has the red, green, and golden yellow Rasta colors and a delightful garlic-flavored dressing.

SALAD

2	cups cooked rice, cooled
2	medium tomatoes, chopped
1	large carrot, peeled and chopped
1	yellow bell pepper, seeded, ribs removed, and chopped
1	cucumber, chopped
1	large yellow onion, peeled and chopped
4	leaves lettuce

DRESSING

4	cloves garlic, peeled
3	green onions, white parts only
1	teaspoon salt
4	ounces soft, silken tofu
¼	cup water
⅓	cup extra-virgin olive oil
2	tablespoons freshly squeezed lemon juice
2	teaspoons Dijon mustard
1	teaspoon lemon zest
1	teaspoon freshly ground black pepper

To prepare the salad: Combine the rice, tomatoes, carrot, bell pepper, cucumber, and onion with the dressing. Place the lettuce leaves on individual salad plates. Mound the salad on top of the leaves.

To prepare the dressing: Place the garlic, green onions, and salt in a food processor and process to blend. Add the tofu and water and process until smooth. With the motor running, pour the oil through the feed tube and blend until creamy. Add the lemon juice, mustard, lemon zest, and black pepper and blend for 30 seconds. Store in an airtight container and refrigerate until ready to use.

AVOCADO, GRAPEFRUIT, AND SPINACH SALAD

MAKES 4 SERVINGS; 1 CUP DRESSING

All varieties of avocados are called pears in the Caribbean. Their delicate flavor and creamy texture contrast beautifully with the leafy spinach and tart, juicy grapefruit in this salad.

SALAD

1	large, firm avocado, peeled, seeded, and sliced
1	large pink grapefruit, peeled, seeded, and divided into sections
6	cups baby spinach leaves

DRESSING

¼	cup grapefruit juice
1	teaspoon honey
½	teaspoon Dijon mustard
1	clove garlic, peeled and minced
⅓	cup olive oil
1	teaspoon salt
1	teaspoon freshly ground black pepper

To prepare the salad: Gently combine the avocado and grapefruit in a small bowl. Chill for 30 minutes.

To prepare the dressing: Meanwhile, whisk together the grapefruit juice, honey, mustard, and garlic in a small bowl. Slowly whisk in the oil. Add the salt and pepper and stir to combine.

Place the spinach leaves on individual serving plates. Mound the avocado mixture on top of the spinach. Pour 3 tablespoons of the dressing over each serving.

Cooking Tip: Use firm, barely ripe avocados. The salad will be mushy if the avocados are too soft.

ISLAND SUPPER SALAD

MAKES 6 SERVINGS

This is a perfect dinner meal for a hot summer night because it can easily be prepared in advance. The Tomatillo Dressing tops it off perfectly.

- 1 cup fresh or frozen peas
- 2 cups pearl barley, cooked and chilled
- 4 ounces mushrooms (any variety), sliced
- 1 large carrot, peeled and chopped
- 1 large purple onion, peeled and thinly sliced
- 1 green bell pepper, seeded, ribs removed, and chopped
- ¼ cup sweet pickle relish
- 1 teaspoon salt
- 1 teaspoon freshly ground black pepper
- ¼ cup Tomatillo Dressing (page 65)

Bring ½ cup water to a boil in a medium saucepan. Add the peas and cook for 2 minutes. Drain.

Combine the peas, barley, mushrooms, carrot, onion, bell pepper, relish, salt, black pepper, and Tomatillo Dressing in a large salad bowl. Chill for 2 to 3 hours before serving to blend the flavors.

MARINATED ONIONS

MAKES 3½ CUPS

Whether you use these onions as a topping for beans or greens or as a condiment for Black Bean and Plantain Fritters (page 72), they're a delicious accent.

- 4 purple onions, peeled and thinly sliced
- 1 teaspoon salt
- ⅛ teaspoon cayenne pepper
- 1¼ cups freshly squeezed lime juice

Place the onions in a shallow bowl. Sprinkle with the salt and pepper. Pour the lime juice over the onions. Stir the ingredients to combine the flavors. Cover and refrigerate for 2 to 3 days.

CALLALOO SOUP

The word callaloo *has many different spellings (*calalu, callilu, *and* calaloo*) and usually refers to the leaves from the taro, coco yam, eddo, or dasheen plant. The soup of the same name has its roots in African cooking. Callaloo is traditionally made with a variety of meats and has the consistency of a bisque. Callaloo leaves are often hard to come by in the United States, but this recipe offers a satisfying substitute.*

¾	pound firm tofu, cut into ½-inch cubes
2	tablespoons hot-pepper sauce
3	tablespoons olive oil
3	ribs celery, chopped
2	cloves garlic, peeled and minced
1	large yellow onion, peeled and chopped
1	jalapeño chile pepper, seeded and finely chopped (wear plastic gloves when handling)
8	ounces okra, stems removed and cut into rounds
4	ounces fresh spinach or Swiss chard, stems removed and blanched
5	cups vegetable broth
1½	cups unsweetened coconut milk
2	sprigs fresh thyme
2	teaspoons salt
2	teaspoons freshly ground black pepper
¼	teaspoon freshly grated nutmeg
4	sprigs fresh cilantro, chopped
	Juice of 1 lime

Marinate the tofu in the hot-pepper sauce in a small bowl for 30 minutes. Set aside.

Heat the oil in a large pot over medium-high heat. Add the celery, garlic, onion, and chile pepper. Sauté the vegetables for 10 minutes, or until tender. Add the okra and spinach or Swiss chard and sauté for 5 minutes. Add the vegetable broth and bring to a boil. Reduce the heat to low and simmer. Add the coconut milk, thyme, salt, black pepper, and nutmeg and simmer for 10 minutes.

Use an immersion blender to thicken the soup to a smooth texture, or remove 2 cups of the soup, place in a food processor, and process until smooth. Pour the blended ingredients back into the pot. Stir to combine. Cover and cook for 40 minutes, stirring occasionally. Add the reserved tofu, cover, and simmer for an additional 10 minutes. Stir in the cilantro and lime juice.

CREOLE BLACK BEAN SOUP

MAKES 6 SERVINGS

Black beans give this soup a hearty texture. The sweet potato provides the broth with a creaminess that blends well with the spices.

1½	cups black beans, soaked (see "Preparing Dried Beans" on page 250)
1	tablespoon butter
1	tablespoon olive oil
2	ribs celery, chopped
2	large carrots, peeled and chopped
1	large yellow onion, peeled and chopped
1	large green bell pepper, seeded, ribs removed, and chopped
1	jalapeño chile pepper, seeded and chopped (wear plastic gloves when handling)
2	bay leaves
1	teaspoon dried thyme
2	tablespoons tomato paste
2½	quarts water
1	large sweet potato, peeled and chopped
2	teaspoons salt
1	teaspoon ground cumin
1	teaspoon chili powder
1	teaspoon freshly ground black pepper
1	cup sweetened coconut milk
4	sprigs fresh cilantro, chopped and stems discarded

Drain the beans. Heat the butter and oil in a large pot over medium-high heat. Add the celery, carrots, onion, bell pepper, chile pepper, bay leaves, and thyme. Sauté for 10 minutes, or until the vegetables are tender. Stir in the tomato paste and cook for 3 minutes, stirring to combine the ingredients.

Add the beans, water, sweet potato, salt, cumin, chili powder, and black pepper. Bring to a boil. Reduce the heat to low, partially cover the pan, and simmer for 20 to 30 minutes, or until the beans are soft.

Remove and discard the bay leaves. Stir in the coconut milk and cilantro. Simmer for an additional 10 minutes.

CARIBBEAN SWEET POTATO BISQUE

MAKES 6 SERVINGS

This smooth, rich, coconut-flavored soup is a delight for the senses.

1½	pounds sweet potatoes, peeled and cubed
4½	cups vegetable broth
½	teaspoon ground turmeric
¾	cup unsweetened coconut milk
1	teaspoon salt
½	teaspoon sugar
¼	teaspoon cayenne pepper
¼	teaspoon ground white pepper
1½	tablespoons olive oil
1	yellow onion, peeled and thinly sliced
1	tablespoon freshly squeezed lime juice

Bring the sweet potatoes and vegetable broth to a boil in a large pot over high heat. Add the turmeric. Reduce the heat to low, cover, and simmer for 15 to 18 minutes, or until the potatoes are tender when pierced with a fork. Strain the potatoes into a food processor, reserving the broth from the pot. Process the potatoes, adding 1 tablespoon of the reserved broth at a time, until the mixture is smooth. Pour the potatoes back into the pot. Stir in the coconut milk, salt, sugar, cayenne pepper, and white pepper. Simmer for 5 to 8 minutes, stirring occasionally.

Heat the oil in a small skillet over medium-high heat. Add the onion and sauté for 10 minutes, or until golden brown. Add the onion and lime juice to the soup. If the soup is too thick, stir in a few more tablespoons of the vegetable broth until the soup is the desired consistency. Serve warm.

BLACK BEAN AND PLANTAIN FRITTERS

MAKES 8 FRITTERS

Black beans and plantains are the perfect combination for this dish. The black bean filling inside the fritter is a delicious surprise.

FILLING

½   cup vegetable oil
2   cloves garlic, peeled and minced
1   medium yellow onion, peeled and chopped
2   cans (15 ounces each) black beans, rinsed, drained, and mashed
1   tablespoon Caribbean hot sauce, such as Pickapeppa, or Vegetarian
    Worcestershire Sauce (page 255)
1   teaspoon dried oregano
1   teaspoon salt
1   teaspoon freshly ground black pepper
⅛   teaspoon cayenne pepper

DOUGH

4   ripe, black plantains
½   cup fresh bread crumbs
    Sour cream (optional)
    Marinated Onions (page 68) optional

To prepare the filling: Heat 1 tablespoon of the oil in a large skillet over medium-high heat. Add the garlic and onion. Sauté for 10 minutes, or until the onions are soft and golden. Add the beans, hot sauce or Worcestershire sauce, oregano, salt, black pepper, and cayenne pepper. Cook for 8 to 10 minutes, stirring occasionally. Remove the pan from the heat.

Place the black bean mixture in a food processor and process to puree. Set aside.

To prepare the plantain dough: Leave the skins on the plantains and rinse them. Place the plantains in a large pot and cover with hot water. Cook the plantains over high heat for 8 to 10 minutes, or until the skins start to open. Carefully drain off the water and allow the plantains to cool. When the plantains are cool enough to handle, peel off the skins. Place the plantains in a food processor. Process until they form a soft dough, adding bread crumbs as necessary to make a workable mixture.

Form the dough into 8 balls, leaving a small amount of dough to use as needed. Flatten the balls into circles, approximately 1-inch thick. Spoon $\frac{1}{4}$ teaspoon of the black-bean mixture into the center of the dough circle. Fold up the edges of the circle to make a ball that encloses the bean mixture, adding pinches of dough to cover the beans, if necessary.

Heat the remaining 7 tablespoons oil in a large skillet over medium-high heat. Place the fritters in the hot oil. Cook the fritters until golden brown on all sides. Reduce the heat to low and cook for an additional 3 to 5 minutes, or until the fritters are cooked through. Serve with sour cream and the Marinated Onions, if desired.

PLANTAIN PATTIES

MAKES 8 PATTIES

Plantains are used in this recipe in the way we sometimes use potatoes in American dishes. I've added a meat substitute to this recipe to make it a completely vegetarian dish. There are several good soybean-based brands on the market, but my personal favorite is the Lite-Life line. I love mixing the ground meat and sausage flavors together in this recipe, but you can use all of one or the other. The brown bits that are left in the bottom of the pan after the patties have been cooked make a terrific gravy.

2	yellow plantains, peeled and cut into chunks
1	large yellow onion, peeled and quartered
1	package (12 ounces) ground beef meat substitute
1	package (12 ounces) sausage meat substitute
2½	teaspoons salt
2½	teaspoons freshly ground black pepper
1	teaspoon African-Style Curry Powder (page 4) or prepared curry powder
½	teaspoon ground allspice
¼	teaspoon freshly grated nutmeg
1	egg
1	cup whole wheat or all-purpose flour
½	cup vegetable oil
½	cup vegetable broth or water
1	tablespoon Caribbean hot sauce, such as Pickapeppa sauce, or Vegetarian Worcestershire Sauce (page 255)

Place the plantains and onion in a food processor and process for 1 minute to chop.

Place the beef substitute and sausage substitute in a large bowl. Add the plantain mixture, 1 teaspoon of the salt, 1 teaspoon of the pepper, the curry powder, allspice, nutmeg, and egg. Mix well to combine. Form the mixture into 8 (3-inch) patties.

Combine the flour, the remaining 1½ teaspoons salt, and the remaining 1½ teaspoons pepper in a shallow container. Lightly dredge the patties in the flour, retaining the flour that is left to use in the gravy.

Heat the oil in a large skillet over medium-high heat until hot but not smoking. Working in batches, fry the patties for 3 to 4 minutes per side, or until golden brown on each side. Remove from the oil to a paper towel–covered plate to drain.

Remove all but 3 tablespoons of the oil from the skillet. Reduce the heat to low. Add 3 tablespoons of the remaining flour to the oil, stirring to loosen any particles on the bottom of the skillet. Stir in a circular motion with the back of a spoon for 5 minutes, or until the mixture is golden, smooth, and bubbly. Slowly stir in the vegetable broth or water. Increase the heat to high, bringing the gravy to a boil. Boil and stir for 1 minute. Add the hot sauce or Worcestershire sauce and the remaining ½ teaspoon each of the salt and pepper. Reduce the heat to low and simmer for 8 minutes, stirring frequently. Serve the gravy over the patties.

PIGEON PEAS AND RICE

This is a classic New Year's day dish in the Caribbean. It's eaten for good luck, as are black-eyed peas in America. Pigeon peas and rice are so good that they've become popular year-round all over the islands.

1	tablespoon butter
1	tablespoon olive oil
3	cloves garlic, peeled and crushed
1	large yellow onion, peeled and chopped
3½	cups vegetable broth
2	bay leaves
2	tablespoons chopped parsley
1	teaspoon dried thyme
1	jalapeño chile pepper, whole (wear plastic gloves when handling)
2½	cups pigeon peas, picked over and soaked
2	cups uncooked long-grain white rice
1	cup unsweetened coconut milk
1	teaspoon ground allspice
1	teaspoon salt
1	teaspoon freshly ground black pepper
⅛	teaspoon cayenne pepper

Heat the butter and oil in a large stew pot. Add the garlic and onion. Sauté for 10 minutes, or until the onion is tender. Increase the heat to high and add the vegetable broth.

Add the bay leaves, parsley, thyme, and chile pepper. Drain the peas in a colander, and stir into the broth.

Bring the mixture back to a boil. Reduce the heat to low and simmer for 45 minutes, stirring occasionally, or until the peas are almost tender but are still slightly firm. Stir in the rice, coconut milk, allspice, salt, black pepper, and cayenne pepper. Simmer for an additional 20 minutes, or until the liquid has been absorbed and the rice and pigeon peas are tender. Remove and discard the chile pepper and bay leaves before serving.

JERK-GRILLED VEGETABLES

MAKES 4 SERVINGS

Using skewers is a great way to cook and serve these spicy grilled vegetables. This method probably originated from the use of sticks or twigs threaded through meats and vegetables and placed over an open fire.

MARINADE

6	green onions, trimmed
1	medium yellow onion, peeled and quartered
¾	cup light soy sauce
½	cup red wine vinegar
¼	cup olive oil
¼	cup packed brown sugar
2	tablespoons Jerk Seasoning (page 62) or prepared jerk seasoning

VEGETABLES

1	medium zucchini, cut into ½-inch thick slices
8	cherry tomatoes, halved
8	medium button mushrooms
8	broccoli florets
2	medium red or yellow bell peppers, seeded, ribs removed, and quartered

To prepare the marinade: Place the green onions and onion in a food processor and process to chop. Add the soy sauce, vinegar, oil, brown sugar, and jerk seasoning and process to grind the ingredients together.

To prepare the vegetables: Soak 8 wooden skewers in water for a few minutes to prevent them from burning. Thread the vegetables onto the skewers, starting with the zucchini and alternating the vegetables. Place the skewers in a large, glass baking dish. Pour the marinade over the skewered vegetables. Marinate in the refrigerator for 2 to 4 hours.

Coat the grill rack with oil. Heat the grill according to the manufacturer's instructions. When the coals are hot, place the skewers on the oiled grill. Cook the vegetables for 4 to 5 minutes per side, or until the vegetables are tender but not burnt.

JERK TOFU

MAKES 6 SERVINGS

Tofu is the perfect vehicle for the spicy jerk seasoning in this recipe. Marinating the tofu infuses the otherwise bland soy product with flavor.

1½	cups vegetable broth
2	pounds firm tofu, sliced
½	teaspoon salt
1	cup barbecue sauce or 'Cueing Sauce (page 161)
¼	cup olive oil
¼	cup packed brown sugar
2	tablespoons Jerk Seasoning (page 62) or prepared jerk seasoning

Bring the vegetable broth to a simmer in a large saucepan over low heat. Add the tofu and salt, and simmer for 5 minutes. Remove the tofu from the pan with a slotted spoon to a paper towel–covered plate to drain.

Combine ½ cup of the barbecue sauce, the oil, brown sugar, and jerk seasoning in a large bowl. Place the tofu in the bowl and toss to coat with the marinade. Marinate the tofu in the refrigerator for 2 hours or overnight.

Preheat the broiler.

Place the tofu on a baking sheet. Brush with the remaining ½ cup barbecue sauce. Broil the tofu for 7 to 10 minutes, or until the top starts to bubble.

Cooking Tip: To make this recipe on the grill, heat the grill according to the manufacturer's instructions. Brush both sides of the tofu with the marinade. Grill the tofu for about 7 minutes per side.

COO COO

The history of this recipe can be traced back to the Indians of Brazil. No one really knows how coo coo *spread to the islands. The preparation of this dish is very similar to that of African mealie (dried corn).* Coo coo *is usually served as a starchy vegetable side dish. I've made a few additions to make it a vegetarian main dish.*

2	tablespoons butter, softened
3	cups water
8	small okra, stems removed and sliced crosswise
1	small onion, peeled and finely chopped
1	green bell pepper, seeded, ribs removed, and chopped
2	cloves garlic, peeled and minced
1	teaspoon salt
¼	teaspoon cayenne pepper
1½	cups cornmeal
4	ounces soft, silken tofu, drained

Lightly grease a 9-inch loaf pan with 1 tablespoon of the butter.

Bring the water to a boil in a heavy saucepan over medium heat. Add the okra, onion, bell pepper, garlic, salt, and cayenne pepper. Cover and cook for 10 minutes. Remove all the vegetables from the water with a slotted spoon and place in a bowl. Set aside.

Return the cooking water to a boil. While stirring rapidly, slowly pour the cornmeal into the water. Cook, stirring constantly, for 5 minutes, or until the mixture is stiff but smooth. Stir in the tofu, the remaining 1 tablespoon butter, and the reserved vegetables. Scrape the *coo coo* into the prepared loaf pan. Allow the *coo coo* to set for 1 hour.

Cut around the edges of the *coo coo* with a sharp knife and turn it out on to a serving plate. Slice before serving.

SPICY ISLAND CORNBREAD

MAKES 9 SERVINGS

This cornbread has a peppery bite and is excellent when served with a bowl of soup or hearty stew on a cold winter's day.

1	cup whole wheat or all-purpose flour
1	cup cornmeal, finely ground
3	tablespoons sugar
1	tablespoon baking powder
½	teaspoon garlic powder
½	teaspoon freshly ground black pepper
½	teaspoon salt
¼	teaspoon cayenne pepper
1	large egg
1	cup plain soy milk
2	ounces soft, silken tofu, drained
¼	cup butter, softened
2	teaspoons hot-pepper sauce
1	teaspoon grated orange zest

Preheat the oven to 400 degrees. Lightly grease a 9-inch baking pan.

Sift the flour, cornmeal, sugar, baking powder, garlic powder, black pepper, salt, and cayenne pepper into a large bowl.

Beat the egg in a food processor or blender. Add the soy milk, tofu, butter, hot-pepper sauce, and orange zest and process to mix well. Add the egg mixture to the flour mixture, stirring until just combined. Spoon the batter into the prepared baking pan.

Bake for 20 minutes, or until golden brown and a toothpick inserted in center of the bread comes out clean.

SWEET CARIBBEAN CORNBREAD

MAKES 12 SERVINGS

The sweetness of this cornbread makes it perfect to serve with a spicy side dish like Jerk Tofu (page 78) or Jerk-Grilled Vegetables (page 77).

1	cup whole wheat or all-purpose flour
¾	cups yellow cornmeal
¼	cup packed dark brown sugar
2	teaspoons baking powder
½	teaspoon salt
½	teaspoon freshly grated nutmeg
½	teaspoon ground cinnamon
½	cup plain soy milk
½	cup sweetened coconut milk
¼	cup butter, melted and cooled
2	eggs, beaten
½	cup shredded unsweetened coconut

Preheat the oven to 400 degrees. Lightly coat an 8-inch baking pan with cooking spray.

Combine the flour, cornmeal, brown sugar, baking powder, salt, nutmeg, and cinnamon in a large bowl.

Combine the soy milk, coconut milk, butter, and eggs in a small bowl. Mix until well-blended. Add the milk mixture to the flour mixture, ½ cup at a time, blending well after each addition. Stir in the coconut. Spread the batter into the prepared baking pan.

Bake for 25 to 30 minutes, or until a toothpick inserted into the center of the cornbread comes out clean and the top is golden brown.

JAMAICAN PLANTATION MUFFINS

MAKES 12 MUFFINS

This recipe is a combination of old and new. Honey and molasses are common ingre-dients in older Jamaican slave recipes. Tofu, a new addition, gives these muffins a nutritious twist.

½	cup firm, silken tofu, drained
1	cup plain soy milk
2	tablespoons vegetable oil
1½	tablespoons honey
2	teaspoons molasses
2	cups whole wheat or all-purpose flour
1	teaspoon baking powder
¾	teaspoon baking soda
½	teaspoon salt
½	teaspoon ground cinnamon

Preheat the oven to 350 degrees. Lightly grease the bottoms of a 12-cup muffin tin.

Place the tofu in a food processor and process to puree. Add the soy milk, oil, honey, and molasses. Process until well-blended.

In a small bowl, combine the flour, baking powder, baking soda, salt, and cinnamon. Add the flour mixture to the tofu mixture, 1 cup at a time, and process to blend gently. (The batter will be thick.) Spoon the batter into the prepared muffin cups until the cups are about three-quarters full.

Bake the muffins for 15 minutes, or until golden brown. Run a sharp knife around the edge of each muffin to loosen them from the cups.

FRUIT AND SWEET POTATO FRITTERS

MAKES 24 FRITTERS

This beautiful combination of fruit and sweet potatoes reflects Caribbean cooks' thrifty use of leftover potatoes and readily available produce.

1	can (16 ounces) sweet potatoes
2	small bananas, peeled and mashed (1 cup)
1	can (8 ounces) crushed pineapple, drained
¼	cup butter, melted
2	tablespoons vanilla extract
1	cup whole wheat or all-purpose flour
1	teaspoon baking powder
½	teaspoon salt
1	teaspoon ground cinnamon
½	teaspoon freshly grated nutmeg
½	cup vegetable oil

Combine the sweet potatoes, bananas, pineapple, butter, and vanilla extract in a large bowl until well-blended.

In another large bowl, sift together the flour, baking powder, and the salt. Gradually add the flour mixture, ½ cup at a time, to the fruit mixture. Stir until smooth. Stir in the cinnamon and nutmeg.

Heat the oil in a deep skillet until hot but not smoking (about 375 degrees). Carefully drop the batter by tablespoonfuls into the oil. Fry the fritters for 30 seconds to 1 minute, or until they turn a light golden brown, turning once to cook evenly. Remove from the oil with a slotted spoon to a paper towel–covered plate to drain.

BAKES

These crispy fried biscuits traveled from the Caribbean islands to the Americas along with slave cooks. Once in America, bakes became known as fried biscuits and were cooked in the grease that was left over after fixing a batch of Southern fried chicken.

2 cups whole wheat or all-purpose flour
2 teaspoons baking powder
2 teaspoons sugar
½ teaspoon salt
2 tablespoons shortening
½ cup cold water
½ cup vegetable oil

Sift together the flour, baking powder, sugar, and salt in a large bowl. With a pastry cutter or fork, cut in the shortening until the mixture is crumbly. Add the water a little at a time, mixing by hand until a soft dough forms. Knead the dough lightly on a floured board, adding a little more flour if it is too sticky. Pinch off walnut-size pieces of the dough and roll them into balls. Flatten the balls into circles about ½ inch thick.

Heat the oil in a heavy skillet over medium heat until hot but not smoking. Fry the bakes, turning once, until golden brown on both sides.

ISLAND BREAD PUDDING

MAKES 8 SERVINGS

A good quality bread that's a day or two old is a perfect foundation for this island delight. Stale bread absorbs the spices and flavorings much better than softer, fresher bread.

2	tablespoons butter
6	slices day-old whole wheat or whole grain bread, cubed
¼	cup raisins
¼	cup dried fruit mix (such as pineapple, mango, orange, and papaya)
1	banana, peeled and sliced
¼	pound soft, silken tofu
2	cups whole vanilla-flavored soy milk
½	cup honey
1	teaspoon freshly squeezed lemon juice
¼	teaspoon freshly grated nutmeg
¼	teaspoon ground cinnamon
¼	teaspoon ground ginger
	Whipped cream (optional)

Preheat the oven to 325 degrees. Lightly grease a 2-quart casserole with the butter. Layer half of the bread on the bottom of the pan. Place half of the raisins, half of the fruit mix, and half of the banana slices in a layer on top of the bread. Place the remaining bread on top of the fruit. Layer the remaining raisins, fruit mix, and banana slices on top of the bread.

Place the tofu in a food processor and process until smooth. Add the soy milk, honey, lemon juice, nutmeg, cinnamon, and ginger and pulse to combine. Slowly pour the soy milk mixture over the bread in the loaf pan. Pierce through the layers with a knife to the bottom of the pan to allow the milk to flow all the way through.

Bake for 45 minutes, or until the pudding is set. Serve hot or cold, topped with whipped cream, if desired.

PLANTAIN GINGERBREAD

MAKES 8 SERVINGS

This unusual gingerbread gives an island twist to an old-fashioned recipe.

- ½ cup sugar
- ½ cup water
- 2 green plantains, peeled and quartered
- 2⅓ cups whole wheat or all-purpose flour
- ½ teaspoon salt
- ½ teaspoon baking soda
- 1 stick butter
- 1 cup molasses
- 1 teaspoon ground ginger
- 1 teaspoon ground cinnamon
- ¼ teaspoon ground cloves
- ¼ teaspoon freshly grated nutmeg
- 1 cup plain soy milk

Preheat the oven to 350 degrees.

Combine the sugar and water in a medium saucepan over medium heat. Bring the mixture to a boil, stirring constantly. Add the plantains and cook for 5 minutes, stirring occasionally. Remove the plantains from the syrup. Discard the syrup. Allow the plantains to cool to room temperature. Slice into rounds.

Grease a 9-inch baking pan. Spread the plantain slices evenly over the bottom of the pan.

Sift the flour, salt, and baking soda together in a large bowl.

Place the butter and molasses in a medium saucepan over medium heat and bring to a boil. Slowly pour the butter mixture into the flour mixture, stirring until smooth. While stirring constantly, add the ginger, cinnamon, cloves, nutmeg, and soy milk. Pour the batter over the plantains in the baking pan. Bake for 50 minutes, or until a toothpick inserted in the middle of the cake comes out clean. Remove the pan to a rack and allow to cool. Run a sharp knife around the edge of the pan to loosen the cake. Turn the cake upside down onto a serving plate. Tap the bottom to loosen the cake from the pan.

Cooking Tip: Plantains look like bananas but have a starchy potato-like texture. As plantains ripen, the fruit becomes sweeter and the skin color changes from green to yellow to half-black and finally to black. Keep plantains at room temperature until you're ready to use them.

CAYMAN MANGO BREAD

MAKES 10 SERVINGS

When mangos are in season, slice them, pack them tightly into a zip-top bag, and freeze them. The mango pieces will keep for up to 3 months, and you'll be able to make this delicious treat any time!

2	mangos, seeded and sliced
¾	cup butter
1¾	cups sugar
¾	cup packed light brown sugar
4	large eggs
1	cup low-fat peach yogurt
1	tablespoon rum-flavored extract
3	cups whole wheat or all-purpose flour
1½	teaspoons baking powder
1½	teaspoons baking soda
1	teaspoon ground coriander
1	teaspoon freshly grated nutmeg
½	teaspoon ground cinnamon
½	teaspoon salt
1	tablespoon orange zest
1	cup sweetened shredded coconut
2	cups chopped pecans

Preheat the oven to 350 degrees. Coat a 12-cup Bundt pan with cooking spray. Lightly flour the pan.

Place the mango slices in a food processor and process to puree. (You should have about 1½ cups.)

Place the butter, sugar, and brown sugar in a food processor or large bowl. Process or mix with an electric mixer on medium speed until creamy. Add the eggs, one at a time. Mix in the yogurt and rum extract.

In a medium bowl, combine the flour, baking powder, baking soda, coriander, nutmeg, cinnamon, and salt with a fork. Add the flour mixture to the sugar mixture, 1 cup at a time, and mix well. Add the mango pulp and orange zest, mixing until well-blended. Stir in the coconut and pecans until just combined. Pour the batter into the prepared Bundt pan. Gently shake the pan to settle the batter evenly.

Bake for 1 hour, or until a toothpick inserted near the center comes out clean. Remove the pan to a rack and allow to cool completely. Run a sharp knife around the edge of the pan to loosen the bread. Invert the bread onto a serving plate. Wrap the bread in plastic wrap or foil and refrigerate until ready to use.

CARIBBEAN *TOTOES*

MAKES 12 SERVINGS

This old-fashioned Jamaican recipe gets a new ethnic vegetarian twist with the inclusion of soy milk.

2	cups self-rising flour
½	teaspoon ground cinnamon
½	teaspoon freshly grated nutmeg
⅛	teaspoon ground allspice
1	cup firmly packed light brown sugar
½	cup butter, softened
1	egg
½	cup vanilla-flavored soy milk
½	tablespoon vanilla extract

Preheat the oven to 400 degrees. Lightly grease a 9-inch baking pan.

Sift together the flour, cinnamon, nutmeg, and allspice in a medium bowl.

With an electric mixer on medium speed, beat the sugar and butter together in a large bowl until creamy. Add the egg, soy milk, and vanilla extract and beat until smooth.

With the mixer on low speed, add the flour mixture to the butter mixture, 1 cup at a time, blending well. Spread the mixture in the prepared baking pan.

Bake for 30 minutes, or until a toothpick inserted in the center comes out clean. Remove the pan to a rack and allow to cool to room temperature. Cut the totoes into 12 squares. Store in an airtight container.

MILK AND PAPAYA DRINK

MAKES 4 SERVINGS

An easy chair and a glass of this refreshing punch will transport you to the Caribbean with every sip.

2   limes
1   small ripe papaya, peeled and coarsely chopped
½   cup vanilla-flavored soy milk
¼   cup sugar
½   cup crushed ice

Grate ½ teaspoon zest from one of the limes. Cut the lime in half and squeeze 3 tablespoons juice into a cup. Reserve the remaining lime.

Place the papaya, soy milk, sugar, ice, lime juice, and lime zest in a food processor or blender. Process to blend until smooth. Serve in chilled glasses. Slice the remaining lime and decorate each glass with one of the slices.

CUCUMBER POWER DRINK

MAKES 8 SERVINGS

The lime juice and ginger add a Caribbean accent to this flavorful drink. I don't drink coffee, so this unusual pick-me-up is the perfect way to start the day!

4	medium cucumbers, chopped (6 cups)
1	piece (1 inch) ginger root, peeled
6	cups water
1	tablespoon freshly squeezed lime juice
1	tablespoon honey

Place the cucumbers, ginger root, and water in a food processor or blender. Process to grind into fine pieces. Strain the cucumber mixture through a fine sieve into a large pitcher. Add the lime juice and honey to the pitcher. Stir well and chill.

MANGO EGGNOG

MAKES 8 SERVINGS

This is a unique alternative to the typical eggnog served during the holidays. It is thick and rich, like the traditional punch, but low in cholesterol.

2	ripe mangos, peeled, pitted, and chopped
4	medium bananas, peeled and chopped
4	cups chilled vanilla-flavored soy milk
¼	cup sugar
4	tablespoons rum extract
2	tablespoons honey
2	teaspoons vanilla extract
1	teaspoon freshly grated nutmeg

Place the mangos, bananas, soy milk, sugar, rum extract, honey, vanilla extract, and ½ teaspoon of the nutmeg in a food processor or blender. Process to blend. Pour the eggnog into a punch bowl. Sprinkle the remaining ½ teaspoon nutmeg over top of the punch.

BARLEY LEMONADE

MAKES 8 SERVINGS

This barley lemonade is a cool, healthy treat after a long day.

SIMPLE SYRUP

- 2 cups sugar
- 1 cup water
- Zest of 1 lemon
- 2 lemons, peeled, sectioned, and seeded

BARLEY LEMONADE

- ½ cup pearl barley
- 3 quarts water

To prepare the simple syrup: Combine the sugar and water in a small saucepan over medium heat. Add the lemon zest and lemon pulp. Boil until the mixture thickens, stirring often. Push the lemon mixture through a fine sieve placed over a bowl. Discard the remaining pulp. Set aside.

To prepare the Barley Lemonade: Combine the barley and water in a medium saucepan over low heat. Bring to a simmer and cook for 30 minutes, or until the water has been reduced by one-third. Pour the barley water through a fine sieve into a large pitcher or jug. Stir in the syrup and refrigerate. Serve over ice.

AFRICAN AND NATIVE AMERICAN VEGETARIAN RECIPES

I HAVE SPECIAL TIES TO NATIVE AMERICAN culture on both sides of my family, including a great-grandfather who was born into slavery but escaped in his youth and was raised by Seminoles in Oklahoma. A Creek word for "free people" or "runaway," Seminole is an especially fitting name for a tribe that included displaced members of several other Native American tribes as well as many escaped African slaves.

In early America, there was extensive contact between Native Americans and African captives—cultures characteristically tied to and sustained by the land, and long accustomed gathering and cultivating a tremendous variety of plants as food. To name just a few of the culinary connections between these groups: The Iroquois and Powhatan shared their methods of cooking beans, corn, and squash; the Narraganset and Penobscot showed the Africans how to make corn pudding and succotash and various ways to use pumpkin and different kinds of melon; Plains tribes taught the Africans how to make jerky; and the tribes of the Southwest offered recipes featuring various chile peppers that were readily embraced by Africans accustomed to the spicy foods of their homelands.

My mother has shared with me a great many childhood memories of Native American foods. She remembers her grandmother preparing beef jerky and hominy. She grew up calling hominy by its Seminole name, *sofky*. Her family ate it with scrambled eggs or as a cold dish, and my mother was especially fond of drinking the sour *sofky* liquid with a little sugar in it. Another of my mother's childhood favorites, *itishca*, was often served at dinner. This dish was made from yellow corn, and my mother remembers how her own mother laid the fresh kernels to dry on white dish towels on the roof of the barn and soon learned to cover the corn with screens to keep the birds from eating it.

Preparing Native American dishes is a wonderful way of paying tribute to the Native Americans who offered us refuge and the resources to survive in America. As the Creek saying goes, *"Hompaks ce!"*—Y'all eat now!

CRANBERRY SAUCE

MAKES 1 CUP

Algonquin tribes prepared cranberry sauce with maple sugar and birch sap, ingredients that many modern cooks would have trouble obtaining. This is a modernized version of their recipe.

1	pound cranberries
	Zest and juice of 3 oranges
1½	cups sugar
½	teaspoon ground ginger
½	teaspoon ground cinnamon
½	teaspoon freshly grated nutmeg
⅛	teaspoon salt

Place the cranberries, orange zest, orange juice, sugar, ginger, cinnamon, nutmeg, and salt in a nonreactive saucepan over low heat. Cook the sauce for 15 to 20 minutes, or until the cranberries soften and pop. Cool and serve.

TRAIL MIX

MAKES 8 SERVINGS

This mixture of seeds, dried fruits, and nuts provided a quick snack or meal as the Native Americans traveled from one place to another. Drying the fruits and salting the nuts helped preserve the mixture.

2	cups air-popped popcorn, lightly salted
1½	cups dried cranberries
1½	cups raisins
1½	cups dried apples
1½	cups dried apricots
½	cup pecans, shelled, toasted, and salted
½	cup walnuts, shelled, toasted, and salted
½	cup peanuts, shelled, toasted, and salted

Combine all ingredients in a large bowl. Evenly divide the mix among individual zip-top plastic bags.

MOHAWK POTATO CHIPS

MAKES 6 SERVINGS

Not many people know that a Mohawk named George Crum invented potato chips. Crum was the chef at Moon Lake Lodge restaurant in Saratoga Springs, New York. The story goes that in 1853, a customer ordered fried potatoes with his meal. The diner kept sending the potatoes back time and again because they weren't crispy enough. Crum decided to slice the potatoes paper-thin, salt them heavily, and refry them. Saratoga Chips soon became a regular menu item at the restaurant.

4	Idaho potatoes, peeled
1½	quarts vegetable oil
1	teaspoon salt
½	cup malt vinegar, optional

With a sharp knife or a mandoline, slice the potatoes about $1/16$ inch thick. You should have 6 cups of potatoes. Place the potato slices in a large colander. Rinse with cold water until the water runs clear. Dry the potatoes in a salad spinner and pat dry with paper towels to remove all excess moisture. (Any remaining water will cause the oil to spatter.)

Heat the oil to 315 degrees in a 6-quart, heavy-bottomed, straight-sided pot to prevent the oil from bubbling over when frying the potatoes. Or, if you don't have a thermometer, drop a small piece of bread into the oil. The oil is the right temperature when the bread turns a light brown and floats to the top after frying for about 2 minutes.

Carefully place one-third of the potatoes at a time in the hot oil. Stir occasionally as they fry to ensure even cooking. Fry the potatoes for 20 minutes, or until light brown. If the potatoes brown in a shorter amount of time, the oil is too hot. The potato slices will either be cooked too much or not cooked enough. Reduce the heat and allow the oil to cool for a minute before adding the next batch of potato slices if the oil is too hot. Repeat frying to use all the potatoes.

Remove the potatoes from the oil with a slotted spoon to a paper towel–covered baking sheet to drain. Salt the chips immediately. Serve with the vinegar, if desired.

GARLIC MOHAWK POTATO CHIPS

MAKES 6 SERVINGS

These spicy garlic-flavored versions of Mr. Crum's famous chips are always a hit as an appetizer.

1	recipe Mohawk Potato Chips (page 98)
3	tablespoons butter
4	sprigs parsley, chopped
2	cloves garlic, peeled and crushed
1	teaspoon salt
1	teaspoon freshly ground black pepper
¼	teaspoon cayenne pepper

Prepare the Mohawk Potato Chips.

Heat the butter in a small saucepan over medium heat until melted. Add the parsley, garlic, salt, black pepper, and cayenne pepper. Cook, stirring, for 1 minute.

Place the potato chips in a large bowl. Pour the garlic sauce over the potato chips. Carefully mix the sauce and chips together with a rubber spatula so that the chips don't break. Serve immediately.

SUNFLOWER SEED SNACKS

MAKES 8 TO 10 CAKES

These little cakes are perfect as an appetizer with a spicy salsa or as a breakfast dish topped with berry jam.

2	cups sunflower seeds, shelled and unsalted
1¾	cups water
2	teaspoons salt
¾	teaspoon freshly ground black pepper
½	cup whole-germ cornmeal
½	cup shortening
	Whole wheat or all-purpose flour

Place the sunflower seeds, water, 1 teaspoon of the salt, and the pepper in a large pot over high heat. Bring the mixture to a boil. Reduce the heat to low and simmer for 1 hour, stirring occasionally. Remove the pot from the heat. Slowly add the cornmeal, 1 tablespoon at a time, stirring until the mixture is smooth and forms a dough. The dough should be stiff and sticky.

Melt the shortening in a large skillet over medium-high heat until hot but not smoking. Dust your hands with a little flour. Take a handful of the dough and pat it into a ½-inch thick cake. Working in batches, place 3 or 4 cakes in the skillet. Do not crowd the cakes in the skillet. Fry until golden brown on each side. Remove from the oil to a paper towel–covered plate to drain. Repeat to make a total of 8 to 10 cakes. Sprinkle the remaining 1 teaspoon salt over the cakes.

WILD GREEN SALAD

MAKES 6 SERVINGS

This tartly flavored combination of greens is attributed to Algonquin tribes. Jerusalem artichokes are nutty-flavored tubers that are members of the sunflower family. They were grown by Native Americans, who called them sunroots, and are similar in texture to potatoes. The maple syrup is a common ingredient in Native American recipes. The sweetness adds a good balance to the peppery greens.

DRESSING

⅔   cup sunflower seed oil
⅓   cup cider vinegar
3   tablespoons maple syrup
1   teaspoon salt
1   teaspoon freshly ground black pepper

SALAD

2   cups watercress
1½   cups dandelion leaves
1   cup thinly sliced Jerusalem artichokes
1   bunch green onions, trimmed and chopped
½   cup Belgian endive
½   cup frisée leaves
½   cup fresh mint leaves
1   cup toasted sunflower seeds

To prepare the dressing: Combine the oil, vinegar, syrup, salt, and pepper in a small bowl.

To prepare the salad: Combine the watercress, dandelion, artichokes, green onions, endive, frisée, and mint in a large salad bowl. Serve on individual salad plates topped with the sunflower seeds and the dressing.

Cooking Tip: You will need commercially grown watercress and dandelion leaves for this recipe. These greens are sometimes difficult to obtain, but spinach, arugula, cos, radicchio, mustard, or purslane greens are good substitutes.

PUMPKIN SOUP

Native Americans made use of all types of winter squash and pumpkins. This creamy soup is a deliciously light first course for a vegetarian Thanksgiving dinner.

1	tablespoon butter
1	tablespoon olive oil
1	green bell pepper, seeded, ribs removed, and chopped
1	small yellow onion, peeled and chopped
2	medium tomatoes, chopped
1	teaspoon dried mint
1	teaspoon salt
1	teaspoon ground white pepper
½	teaspoon sugar
½	teaspoon freshly grated nutmeg
1	can (15 ounces) pumpkin
2	cups vegetable broth
½	cup light cream
1	tablespoon whole wheat or all-purpose flour
¼	cup pine nuts, toasted (see "Toasting Nuts and Seeds" on page 252)

Heat the butter and oil in a large stock pot over medium-high heat. Add the bell pepper and onion and sauté for 5 minutes, or until the vegetables are tender. Add the tomatoes, mint, salt, white pepper, sugar, and nutmeg. Cook, stirring, for 2 to 3 minutes. Add the pumpkin and vegetable broth. Reduce the heat to low and simmer for 20 minutes, stirring occasionally.

Combine the cream and flour in a small bowl until smooth. Increase the heat to high and bring the soup to a boil. Stir the cream mixture into the soup. Reduce the heat to low and bring to a simmer. Cook the soup for 3 minutes, stirring occasionally. Serve topped with the pine nuts.

ALGONQUIN WILD NUT SOUP *(PAGANENS)*

MAKES 6 SERVINGS

This soup is another example of the Native American way of living off the land. Nuts are an unusual soup ingredient now, but it was fairly common to use them this way hundreds of years ago.

6	cups vegetable broth
4	cups hazelnuts, shelled and crushed
6	shallots, peeled and chopped
3	tablespoons chopped parsley
1	teaspoon salt
1	teaspoon freshly ground black pepper

Place the vegetable broth, hazelnuts, shallots, parsley, salt, and pepper in a large stock pot over high heat and bring to a boil. Reduce the heat to low and simmer slowly for 1 to 1½ hours, stirring occasionally. Serve with Hot Water Cornbread (page 113) or Indian Fry Bread (page 116).

HOMINY STEW

MAKES 8 SERVINGS

This stew is also called posole. *Some Native American tribes call the combination of corn, beans, and squash the Three Sisters because these vegetables are often planted together. The cornstalks support the bean vines, and the squash vines help keep the field free of weeds.*

2	tablespoons olive oil
1	medium yellow onion, peeled and chopped
1	medium green bell pepper, seeded, ribs removed, and chopped
1	medium zucchini, chopped
2	cloves garlic, peeled and minced
1	medium Yukon gold or Irish potato, scrubbed and chopped
1	can (15 ounces) hominy
1	tablespoon dried oregano
1	tablespoon chili powder
½	teaspoon freshly ground black pepper
½	teaspoon salt
1	can (15 ounces) chipotle chile peppers, chopped
4	cups vegetable broth
1	can (15 ounces) red kidney beans, rinsed and drained
½	pound fresh spinach, chopped
¼	cup tomato paste

Heat the oil in a large stock pot over medium-high heat. Add the onion, bell pepper, zucchini, and garlic and sauté for 10 minutes, or until the vegetables are tender. Add the potato, hominy, oregano, chili powder, black pepper, salt, chile peppers, and vegetable broth. Stir to combine. Cook for 20 to 25 minutes, stirring occasionally.

Stir in the beans, spinach, and tomato paste. Simmer for 15 minutes, stirring occasionally. Remove from the heat and set aside for 5 minutes before serving.

Cooking Tip: Hominy is dried corn and can be found in the canned vegetable aisle in most grocery stores.

CORN PUDDING

The Narraganset and Penobscot tribes taught African slaves how to make corn pudding. It's easy to make, creamy, and filling. While corn pudding is traditionally served as a side dish, I see no reason why it shouldn't have the starring role in a vegetarian meal.

5	tablespoons butter, softened
2	large eggs
1	cup whole milk or heavy cream
3	tablespoons sugar
2	tablespoons whole wheat or all-purpose flour
½	teaspoon salt
½	teaspoon freshly ground black pepper
½	teaspoon freshly grated nutmeg
2	cups fresh or frozen and thawed corn kernels

Preheat the oven to 350 degrees. Lightly grease a 1-quart casserole with 1 tablespoon of the butter. Melt the remaining 4 tablespoons butter in a cup in the microwave for 10 seconds. Set the butter aside to cool.

Beat the eggs in a food processor or in a large bowl by hand. Add the butter, milk or cream, and sugar, mixing well. Add the flour, salt, pepper, and nutmeg and mix well. Add the corn, mixing well.

Pour the pudding into the prepared casserole. Bake for 45 minutes to 1 hour, or until the custard is set and a knife inserted in the center comes out clean.

GREEN CHILE SQUARES

MAKES 6 SERVINGS

Native Americans in the Southwest made a culinary art of roasting chile peppers. Hatch, New Mexico, home of the Hatch Chile Festival, is known as the chile capital of the world. More than 30,000 acres of chiles are grown there. This simple-to-prepare dish makes a great breakfast or a delicious supper when stuffed inside of a piece of Indian Fry Bread (page 116) or folded into a taco.

2	tablespoons butter, softened
1	small yellow onion, peeled and thinly sliced
1	jar (19 ounces) roasted Anaheim, New Mexican, or poblano chile peppers, drained and cut into strips (wear plastic gloves when handling)
1	block (12 ounces) sharp Cheddar cheese, cut into 12 slices
1	dozen eggs
¼	cup plain soy milk
2	tablespoons whole wheat or all-purpose flour
2	teaspoons salt

Preheat the oven to 350 degrees. Grease the bottom and sides of a 13 × 9-inch baking pan with the butter.

Alternate layers of the onion, peppers, and cheese in the prepared baking pan.

Combine the eggs, soy milk, flour, and the salt in a large bowl. Pour the egg mixture over the onion mixture in the baking dish.

Bake for 10 to 12 minutes, or until the eggs are firm and set. Cut into squares.

MAPLE BAKED BEANS

Some people believe baked beans were created by Native Americans long before anyone in Boston served them. I don't know who invented this dish first, but it's delicious!

4	cups water
1	pound navy or lima beans, picked over and rinsed
1	tablespoon butter
1	medium yellow onion, peeled and sliced
1	cup maple syrup
1½	teaspoons salt
1	teaspoon dry mustard
1	teaspoon ground ginger

Preheat the oven to 350 degrees.

Place the water and beans in a large pot over high heat. Bring to a boil. Reduce the heat to low, cover, and simmer for 2 hours, stirring occasionally. Drain the beans, reserving 2 cups of the cooking liquid. Add water to the beans, if necessary, to make 2 cups.

Melt the butter in a small skillet over medium-high heat. Add the onion and sauté for 10 minutes, or until tender and golden.

Place the beans and reserved cooking liquid in a 3-quart baking dish. Add the onion, maple syrup, salt, mustard, and ginger and stir to combine. Tightly cover the dish with foil. Bake for 2 hours. Uncover and bake for an additional 30 to 45 minutes, or until all the liquid is absorbed. Let stand 10 minutes before serving.

ONION MUSHROOM CORN PONE WITH BATTER-DIPPED GREENS

MAKES 6 SERVINGS

I thought I had heard of recipes for all manner of batter-covered vegetables until I found this Native American recipe for batter-dipped greens. It's a tasty way to serve hardy greens like mustards and collards. The battered greens are especially delicious with the Onion Mushroom Corn Pone, or Native American Polenta, if you prefer a more elegant name.

ONION MUSHROOM CORN PONE

1¼	cups vegetable broth
1	cup plain soy milk
1	cup cornmeal
2	tablespoons butter
1	yellow onion, peeled and thinly sliced
2	cloves garlic, peeled and minced
3–4	ounces assorted mushrooms (such as morels, chanterelles, and oysters), sliced
1	teaspoon cider vinegar
1½	tablespoons minced fresh rosemary
1	teaspoon salt
1	teaspoon freshly ground black pepper

BATTER-DIPPED GREENS

3	cups peanut oil
1	cup whole wheat or all-purpose flour
2	teaspoons salt
1	teaspoon freshly ground black pepper
1	teaspoon baking powder
½	teaspoon cornstarch
⅛	teaspoon cayenne pepper
¼	cup ice water
1	pound mustard or collard greens, stems removed

To prepare the Onion Mushroom Corn Pone: Pour 1 cup of the vegetable broth and the soy milk into a medium saucepan and bring to a boil over medium-high heat. Slowly add the cornmeal, stirring constantly to prevent lumps from forming. Reduce the heat to medium and cook for an additional 20 minutes, stirring often, or until the mixture is creamy. Place in a serving bowl.

Meanwhile, melt the butter in a large saucepan over medium heat. Add the onion and garlic and sauté for 10 minutes, or until tender. Add the mushrooms and sauté for an additional 3 to 5 minutes. Add the remaining $\frac{1}{4}$ cup vegetable broth, the vinegar, rosemary, salt, and pepper. Reduce the heat to low and simmer, stirring occasionally, until smoothly blended. Place in the bowl with the cornmeal mixture. Keep warm.

To prepare the Batter-Dipped Greens: Heat the oil in a large deep-sided skillet until it is hot but not smoking. Combine the flour, 1 teaspoon of the salt, the black pepper, baking powder, cornstarch, and cayenne pepper in a large bowl. Slowly stir in the water until the mixture becomes a thin batter. Dip the greens into the batter, a leaf at a time, shaking off the excess batter. Working in batches, fry the greens in the hot oil. Cook for 1 minute, or until the greens turn a golden brown. Remove from the oil to a paper towel–covered plate to drain. Sprinkle the remaining 1 teaspoon salt over the greens. Serve immediately over the corn pone.

WINTER SQUASH STUFFED WITH PINE NUT DRESSING

MAKES 8 SERVINGS

This dish makes a beautiful presentation and is wonderful for Thanksgiving day.

DRESSING

1	stick butter
2	cloves garlic, peeled and minced
2	ribs celery, chopped
1	large yellow onion, peeled and chopped
1	large green or red bell pepper, seeded, ribs removed, and chopped
3–4	ounces assorted mushrooms (such as buttons, morels, chanterelles, or oysters), sliced (1 cup)
2	cups coarse, dried bread crumbs
2	cups cornbread crumbs
1	cup shelled, roasted pine nuts
2	sprigs fresh thyme, leaves only, chopped
1½	teaspoons crumbled dried sage
1	teaspoon salt
1	teaspoon freshly ground black pepper
1	teaspoon chopped fresh rosemary
1	egg, beaten
1	cup vegetable broth

SQUASH OR PUMPKINS

8	mini winter squash or pumpkins (such as Sweet Dumplings or Jack-be-Littles), halved lengthwise
2	tablespoons vegetable oil
1	cup Cranberry Sauce (page 97) or prepared cranberry sauce, optional

To prepare the dressing: Melt the butter in a large skillet over medium heat. Add the garlic, celery, onion, bell pepper, and mushrooms. Sauté for 10 minutes, or until the vegetables soften.

Add the bread crumbs, cornbread crumbs, pine nuts, thyme, sage, salt, black pepper, and rosemary to the vegetable mixture. Cook, stirring, for 2 to 3 minutes. Remove from the heat. Stir in the egg. Add the vegetable broth, $\frac{1}{4}$ cup at a time, until the stuffing is moist but not wet.

To prepare the squash or pumpkins: Preheat the oven to 375 degrees.

Scoop the seeds and fibers out of the squash or pumpkins, leaving about $\frac{1}{3}$ inch shell. (You may want to reserve the seeds for toasting; see "Toasting Nuts and Seeds" on page 252.) Brush the cut surfaces with a thin film of the oil. Place the squash or pumpkin, cut side up, on a sheet pan. Mound about $\frac{1}{4}$ cup of the dressing into each squash or pumpkin half.

Bake for 30 to 45 minutes, or until the squash is soft and wrinkled. Serve with the cranberry sauce, if desired.

Cooking Tip: To make Winter Squash Stuffed with Squash–Pine Nut Dressing, boil the whole squash in a large pot of water for 5 minutes to soften. Rinse the squash under cold water. Halve the squash lengthwise and scoop out the pulp with a pointed spoon. Chop the pulp and sauté it along with the other vegetables in the dressing.

SUCCOTASH

Succotash is called Msickquatash *by Native Americans in the northeastern United States. The recipe is one of which both Native Americans and many African slave cooks had common knowledge. The ingredients are similar to the African recipe for samp (page 41). The "stewing" method of preparing the dish was also familiar to African captives.*

1	cup dried baby lima beans
1	cup water
1	green bell pepper, seeded, ribs removed, and chopped
1	can (15 ounces) stewed tomatoes
1	cup fresh or frozen and thawed corn kernels
2	small bay leaves
1	tablespoon sugar
1	teaspoon salt
1	teaspoon freshly ground black pepper
½	teaspoon dried thyme
¼	teaspoon cayenne pepper
1	tablespoon butter

Bring a large pot of salted water to a boil over medium heat. Add the beans, making sure the water covers the beans. Cook at a low boil for 18 to 20 minutes, or until almost tender. Drain the beans in a colander.

Combine the beans, water, bell pepper, tomatoes (with juice), corn, bay leaves, sugar, salt, black pepper, thyme, and cayenne pepper in the same large pot over medium-high heat. Bring to a boil. Reduce the heat to medium.

Cook for 8 to 10 minutes, stirring occasionally, or until the corn is tender and the water is almost evaporated. Add the butter and stir gently until it melts over the vegetables. Remove and discard the bay leaves before serving.

HOT WATER CORNBREAD

My mother often made this recipe. I didn't realize it when I was a child, but the bread that we routinely ate during dinner was a Native American recipe. It was often the main meal for many of my African ancestors during slavery.

1½	cups cornmeal
2	tablespoons whole wheat or all-purpose flour
1	tablespoon baking powder
1½	teaspoons sugar
¾	teaspoon salt
1½	cup boiling water
⅓	cup vegetable oil

Combine the cornmeal, flour, baking powder, sugar, and salt in a large bowl. Stirring constantly, slowly pour a steady, thin stream of the boiling water into the bowl. Mix well. The mixture should be soft and smooth, but not too wet.

Heat the oil in a heavy skillet over high heat until hot but not smoking (about 375 degrees). Drop ⅓ cup of the batter into the skillet, making 2½-inch round cakes, about ½ inch thick. Reduce the heat to medium and fry the cornbread for 3 to 4 minutes on each side, or until golden brown.

BLACK WALNUT BREAD WITH SUNFLOWER SEED GRAVY

MAKES 6 SERVINGS (2 CUPS GRAVY)

This moist bread is a creation of the Apache nation and is traditionally served with sunflower gravy. The nuts and seeds provide protein.

BLACK WALNUT BREAD

2	cups black walnuts
1	teaspoon salt
1⅔	cups fresh corn kernels (about 2 to 3 ears of corn) or frozen and thawed
½	cup plain soy milk
2	tablespoons honey
1	package cornhusks, soaked until moist and pliable, or green husks from fresh corn

SUNFLOWER SEED GRAVY

⅓	cup shelled and unsalted sunflower seeds
1	tablespoon butter
1	tablespoon vegetable oil
2	tablespoons cornmeal
2	cups water
1	teaspoon salt

To prepare the Black Walnut Bread: Preheat the oven to 325 degrees. Place the walnuts and salt in a food processor and process until coarsely ground. Set aside.

Combine the corn and soy milk in a large bowl. Add the walnut mixture and honey and stir until well-combined.

Line a 9 × 5 × 3-inch pan with cornhusks, overlapping the edges of the husks to make a continuous lining and to prevent the batter from leaking through. Reserve enough cornhusks for topping. Scrape the batter into the pan. Cover the top of the batter with the remaining corn husks.

Bake for 2 hours. Serve hot like a spoon bread or allow it to cool until firm and cut into squares.

To prepare the Sunflower Seed Gravy: Meanwhile, place the sunflower seeds in a food processor and process for 10 to 15 seconds.

Heat the butter and the oil in a medium skillet over high heat. Add the sunflower seeds and cornmeal, stirring to combine. Slowly add the water, stirring constantly. Bring to a boil to thicken the mixture. Reduce the heat to low and stir in the salt. Top the bread with the gravy just before serving.

Cooking Tip: You can find packages of cornhusks, used for making tamales, in Latino markets if they are not readily available in your local grocery. If using fresh corn, save the corn milk and combine it with the soy milk. Save the green husks from the fresh corn and place them in a plastic bag to keep them from drying out until you are ready to use them.

INDIAN FRY BREAD

MAKES 8 SERVINGS

Native Americans taught Africans how to prepare fry bread, thin rounds of dough made from water or milk, flour, and salt. I first ate fry bread at a Yankton Sioux reservation in South Dakota during a feast they held in the late 1980s. It's delightful served with Green Chile Squares (page 106) or Algonquin Wild Nut Soup (page 103).

4	cups whole wheat or all-purpose flour
1	tablespoon baking powder
1	teaspoon salt
2	cups buttermilk or warm water
1½	quarts vegetable oil

Sift together the flour, baking powder, and salt in a large bowl. Add the buttermilk or water in small amounts, working it into the flour with your hands until a soft, elastic dough forms. Add a little more flour if the dough is too sticky or a little more buttermilk or water if the dough is too stiff.

Knead the dough on a lightly floured surface for 5 minutes. Fold the outer edges of the dough in toward the center. Return the dough to the bowl, cover the bowl with a clean dish towel, and let it rest in a draft-free place for about 30 minutes, or until doubled in size.

Shape the dough into 16 peach-size balls. Traditionally, the dough is stretched out with your hands, but you may use a rolling pin to stretch out the dough on a lightly floured board. Roll each ball out to ½-inch thickness, or ¼-inch thickness for crispier bread. Place the dough between your hands and pat it from hand to hand like you would pizza dough or a tortilla, until it has stretched to 8 to 12 inches in diameter. Repeat this process with each ball of dough.

Heat the oil in a large, heavy-bottomed skillet over high heat until hot but not smoking (about 375 degrees). Poke an air hole in the center of the dough to prevent it from bursting during the frying process. To avoid spattering the oil, carefully slip the dough into the frying pan. Cook for 1 to 2 minutes, or until the dough turns golden brown and puffy with air bubbles. Use a long-handled fork to turn the bread over. Cook for an additional 1 to 2 minutes, or until the bread turns golden brown.

BAKED APPLES

MAKES 6 SERVINGS

Native Americans cored and stuffed apples, wrapped them in wet leaves, and set them on hot rocks to steam beside the fire.

6	baking apples (such as Cortlands, Winesaps, Baldwins, or Rome Beauties)
½	cup maple syrup
3	tablespoons dried cranberries
3	tablespoons raisins
1	tablespoon chopped pecans
2	tablespoons walnut or vegetable oil

Preheat the oven to 375 degrees.

Core the apples, leaving the bottoms intact to form a cavity.

Combine the syrup, cranberries, raisins, and pecans in a small bowl. Place the apples on a baking sheet. Fill the apples with the fruit-and-nut mixture. Drizzle with the oil.

Bake for 30 minutes, or until the apples are tender. Remove from the oven and let the apples stand for 10 to 15 minutes before serving. Serve hot.

INDIAN PUDDING

Today, this dish is usually served as a dessert. Years ago, Native Americans served the pudding with meat and vegetables as part of their midday meal. This modernized version retains the historic recipe's flavor and spirit.

2–3	teaspoons butter
⅔	cup cornmeal
½	teaspoon ground ginger
¼	teaspoon freshly grated nutmeg
4	cups vanilla-flavored soy milk
1	cup maple syrup
¼	cup butter
1½	cup raisins
	Whipped cream (optional)

Preheat the oven to 300 degrees. Lightly grease a 2-quart casserole with butter.

Combine the cornmeal, ginger, and nutmeg in a small bowl.

Combine 3 cups of the milk and the maple syrup in a large saucepan over medium heat. Bring to a boil. Immediately reduce the heat to medium and stir in the ¼ cup butter.

Slowly add the cornmeal mixture to the milk mixture in the saucepan, stirring constantly to prevent lumps. Reduce the heat to low and cook for 5 minutes, stirring constantly as the mixture thickens. Stir in the raisins. Spoon the mixture into the prepared casserole. Pour the remaining 1 cup milk over the pudding. Do not stir.

Bake for 2½ hours, or until the top is golden brown and all the milk has been absorbed. Serve warm, topped with whipped cream, if desired.

MAPLE TEA

MAKES 4 SERVINGS

This tea has a sweet, soothing flavor and is a great eye-opener in the morning.

4   cups water
2   tablespoons maple syrup

Combine the water and maple syrup in a small pot. Bring to a boil over high heat. Cover with a tight-fitting lid and remove the pot from the heat. Allow the tea to steep for 4 minutes. Drink warm.

SEMINOLE ORANGE DRINK

MAKES 4 SERVINGS

Spanish settlers planted the first Seville orange trees grown in Florida and included citrus fruits in their diet to prevent scurvy. Seminoles incorporated the bitter-tasting oranges into recipes such as this unusual and refreshing drink.

6   pimientos, chopped
4   Seville oranges, peeled and sectioned
1   quart orange juice
1   tablespoon freshly squeezed lime juice
1   teaspoon hot-pepper sauce

Place the pimientos and oranges in a pitcher. Add the orange juice, lime juice, and hot-pepper sauce and stir to blend. Refrigerate to chill but do not serve over ice cubes.

Cooking Tip: Seville oranges are often hard to come by, but other types of orange juices and oranges, such as tangelos, blood oranges, or navel oranges, are good substitutes.

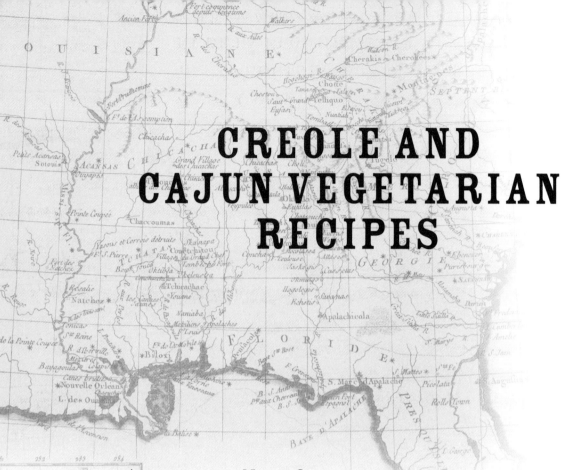

CREOLE AND CAJUN VEGETARIAN RECIPES

A VISIT TO NEW ORLEANS IS LIKE STEPPING into the heart of the ethnic vegetarian experience. It's easy to taste the African influence on its cuisine, from the use of spicy peppers to the way rice is incorporated into many of the recipes. And with so many rich seasonings to choose from, it's easy to translate even the most traditional meat-based dishes into a vegetarian feast. Simply put, the food is world-famous for a reason—it's absolutely glorious.

My husband, Michael, and I visited the French Quarter several years ago to see our friend, Coleen C. Salley, a professor at the University of New Orleans and one of the best storytellers around. Every meal was long and leisurely, steeped in rich flavors and regional tradition, and accompanied by Colleen's vivid accounts of the city's incredible history.

New Orleans' rich cuisine reflects a blend of French, Spanish, Haitian, and African flavors. Two distinct styles have emerged, Creole and Cajun.

The term *Creole* refers to a sophisticated style of cooking strongly influenced by the French settlers who fled Haiti (then Saint-Domingue) in the late 1700s as well as the Spanish, who controlled the Louisiana territory until the early 1800s. American Creole food is easily distinguished from Caribbean Creole by much heavier use of butter, cream, celery, and basil.

Cajun cooking, on the other hand, is famed for its liberal use of hot seasonings like cayenne pepper. This bayou cuisine originated when French peasants from Acadia (now Nova Scotia) fled to Louisiana. Their bold cooking style was incorporated into the local blend of African, French, and Spanish recipes, and Cajun cuisine was born.

Food writer John Egerton has described these two cuisines as being "like city and country cousins, the one rich, elegant, and sophisticated, the other earthy, spicy, straightforward—and both of them superior."

Bon appétit!

▪ CONDIMENTS, APPETIZERS, AND SALADS ▪

▪ SOUPS AND STEWS ▪

▪ MAIN DISHES ▪

▪ BREADS AND DESSERTS ▪

CAJUN SPICE MIX

MAKES ABOUT ¾ CUP

This spicy mix adds a burst of flavor to many recipes.

- 2½ tablespoons ground paprika
- 2 tablespoons salt
- 2 tablespoons garlic powder
- 1 tablespoon freshly ground black pepper
- 1 tablespoon onion powder
- 1 tablespoon cayenne pepper
- 1 tablespoon dried oregano
- 1 tablespoon dried thyme

Combine all ingredients in an airtight container. Shake to mix. Store in a cool, dry place.

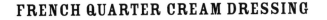

FRENCH QUARTER CREAM DRESSING

MAKES ⅓ CUP

The French influence is evident in every ingredient in this recipe. The creaminess of the dressing is the perfect accent for a mixed green salad, crisp green beans, or asparagus.

- ⅓ cup heavy cream, chilled
- 1 tablespoon white wine vinegar
- 1 tablespoon spicy mustard
- 2 tablespoons olive oil

Pour the cream into a food processor or large bowl. Process or beat with an electric mixer on high speed until thick and creamy. Whisk the vinegar and mustard into the cream until stiff peaks form. Slowly whisk in the oil until the mixture is well-combined. Store in an airtight container in the refrigerator.

CREOLE VINAIGRETTE

MAKES ABOUT 1 CUP

This spicy vinaigrette is one of the main ingredients for Crescent City Potato Salad (page 130) and the perfect dressing for a crisp green salad.

- ¼ cup red wine vinegar
- 1 clove garlic, peeled and crushed
- 1 tablespoon spicy mustard
- 1 teaspoon Cajun Spice Mix (page 123) or prepared Cajun spice mix
- ¾ cup olive oil

Combine the vinegar, garlic, mustard, and Cajun Spice Mix in a small bowl. Slowly whisk in the oil until the mixture thickens. Store in an airtight container in the refrigerator. The vinaigrette will keep for up to 10 days.

NEW ORLEANS ORANGE SAUCE

MAKES ABOUT 1½ CUPS

Try a few spoonfuls of this fabulous sauce on a buttery baked sweet potato for a deliciously different side dish.

- 12 ounces orange marmalade
- 1 tablespoon spicy prepared mustard
- 1½ teaspoons prepared horseradish
- 1 teaspoon freshly squeezed lemon juice

Combine all ingredients in a food processor. Process until blended. Refrigerate for 3 hours and serve at room temperature.

OLIVE SALAD

MAKES ABOUT 6½ CUPS

This piquant salad is a breeze to prepare and incredibly versatile. It also keeps very well, so enjoy it on its own and then use leftovers as a sandwich topping or to make Olive and Pasta Salad (page 128), Muffuletta Salad (page 129), Olive and Chickpea Salad (page 129)—or all of the above!

1	jar (19 ounces) roasted red bell peppers, drained and oil reserved
1	cup pitted black olives
1	cup pimiento-stuffed green olives
1	cup pickled cauliflower and sweet peppers
1	jar (6½ ounces) artichoke hearts
2	medium carrots, ends trimmed
2	ribs celery
2	cloves garlic, peeled
1	small purple onion, peeled and quartered
⅔	cup red wine vinegar
⅔	cup olive oil
1	tablespoon capers
1	tablespoon Italian seasoning
1	teaspoon freshly ground black pepper

Place the roasted peppers, black olives, green olives, cauliflower and sweet peppers, and artichoke hearts (with juice) in a food processor. Pulse for about 30 seconds to chop finely. Do not puree the ingredients. Remove to a small bowl.

Place the carrots, celery, garlic, and onion in the food processor. Pulse for about 30 seconds to chop finely. Do not puree the ingredients. Add the onion mixture to the olive mixture in the bowl and mix well.

Combine the roasted pepper oil, vinegar, olive oil, capers, Italian Seasoning, and black pepper in another small bowl. Pour the oil mixture over the olive mixture. Mix well. Store in an airtight container. Refrigerate for 24 hours before using. Stir the contents occasionally to blend the ingredients. The olive salad will keep in the refrigerator for 10 days.

CRUDITÉS WITH JEZEBEL SAUCE

MAKES 24 SERVINGS

I've made an ethnic-vegetarian—style appetizer out of the standard crudités plate by adding this delightful version of a recipe for Jezebel sauce. I'm not sure how this sauce got its name. Perhaps it refers to the evil queen in the Old Testament. This sauce is both sweet and hot, so it evokes descriptions of heaven and hell! The lettuce leaves become the serving "dish," allowing your guests to eat the entire appetizer.

JEZEBEL SAUCE

- 1 jar (10 ounces) apple jelly
- 1 jar (10 ounces) peach preserves
- 1 tablespoon prepared horseradish
- 1 tablespoon honey
- 1½ teaspoons dry mustard
- ½ teaspoon salt
- ½ teaspoon freshly ground black pepper

CREAM CHEESE SPREAD

- 8 ounces cream cheese, softened
- 8 ounces soft, silken tofu, drained
- 1 teaspoon salt
- 1 teaspoon freshly ground black pepper
- ½ teaspoon cayenne pepper

CRUDITÉS

- 1 small head Belgian endive, leaves separated
- 2 small heads escarole, inner leaves only, separated
- 1 head (3 to 4 ounces) radicchio, leaves separated
- 2 boxes (5 ounces each) melba toast

To prepare the Jezebel Sauce: Combine the jelly, preserves, horseradish, honey, mustard, salt, and the pepper in a small bowl. Cover and refrigerate for at least 8 hours before using.

To prepare the Cream Cheese Spread: Combine the cream cheese, tofu, salt, black pepper, and cayenne pepper in a food processor or small bowl. Process or beat with an electric mixer on medium speed until well-combined. Refrigerate for 30 minutes before using.

To prepare the Crudités: Place the leaves in an alternating pattern on a large serving dish. Place a piece of the melba toast in the center of each leaf. Mound 1 to 2 tablespoons of the cream cheese mixture over the toast. Drizzle 1 to 2 tablespoons of the sauce over the cream cheese mixture. Serve immediately.

OLIVE AND PASTA SALAD

Olive Salad (page 125) brings wonderful zing to cooked penne pasta. Just toss with toasted sesame seeds and fresh Parmesan, and everyone will love this departure from ordinary pasta salad. Best to make a double batch so you can serve seconds!

½	pound penne pasta
4	medium tomatoes, chopped
6	leaves fresh basil, torn
1½	cups Olive Salad (page 125)
¼	cup olive oil
1	cup (4 ounces) freshly grated Parmesan cheese
¼	cup sesame seeds, toasted
2	tablespoons balsamic vinegar
½	teaspoon salt
½	teaspoon freshly ground black pepper
⅛	teaspoon cayenne pepper

Prepare the pasta according to package directions. Drain and cool. Place the pasta in a large bowl. Add the tomatoes, basil, Olive Salad, and oil and toss to combine. Sprinkle with the cheese, sesame seeds, vinegar, salt, black pepper, and cayenne pepper and toss gently to combine.

MUFFULETTA SALAD

MAKES 6 SERVINGS

Muffuletta is a specialty sandwich that originated in New Orleans in the early 1900s. Reinterpreting muffuletta as a salad, I've replaced the crusty Italian bread that's traditionally used for the sandwich with tangy sourdough croutons.

8	ounces lettuce greens (Bibb, Romaine, or Iceberg), torn
8	ounces baby spinach leaves
½	cup Olive Salad (page 125)
¼	cup (1 ounce) freshly grated provolone cheese
¼	cup (1 ounce) freshly grated mozzarella cheese
1	cup sourdough or garlic-flavored croutons
2	tablespoons balsamic vinegar
1	teaspoon salt
1	teaspoon freshly ground black pepper

Combine the lettuce, spinach, and Olive Salad in a large bowl. Add the provolone, mozzarella, croutons, vinegar, salt, and pepper and toss gently to combine.

OLIVE AND CHICKPEA SALAD

MAKES 6 SERVINGS

Here's another wonderful way to serve Olive Salad. The chickpeas marry nicely with the salad, and the feta cheese adds just the right zip.

2	cans (15 ounces each) chickpeas, rinsed and drained
1	cup Olive Salad (page 125)
12	cherry tomatoes, halved
4	sprigs flat-leaf parsley, chopped
1¼	cups (5 ounces) feta cheese, cubed
1	cup sourdough or garlic-flavored croutons
2	tablespoons balsamic vinegar
1	teaspoon salt
1	teaspoon freshly ground black pepper

Combine the chickpeas, Olive Salad, tomatoes, and parsley in a large bowl. Add the cheese, croutons, vinegar, salt, and pepper and toss gently to combine.

CRESCENT CITY POTATO SALAD

MAKES 6 SERVINGS

New Orleans is called the Crescent City because it's located at the bend of the Missis-sippi River. You can see the crescent shape if you look at the location of the city on a map. Louisiana is also famous for its spicy hot sauces. A few dashes of Tabasco or your favorite hot sauce definitely wakes up this unusual salad.

10	medium fingerling or boiling potatoes, scrubbed and quartered
1	cup Creole Vinaigrette (page 124)
4	green onions, trimmed and finely chopped
2	ribs celery, chopped
1	red bell pepper, seeded, ribs removed, and chopped
1	green bell pepper, seeded, ribs removed, and chopped
1	small purple onion, peeled and chopped
6	sprigs flat-leaf parsley, chopped
1	teaspoon salt
1	teaspoon freshly ground black pepper
1 or 2	dashes hot-pepper sauce

Place the potatoes in a large saucepan. Cover with boiling water. Cook the potatoes for 15 to 20 minutes, or until tender when pierced with a fork. Drain the potatoes in a large colander and allow to cool slightly. Cut the potatoes into 1/2 inch-thick slices. Place in a large bowl.

Pour the Creole Vinaigrette over the potatoes, 1/4 a cup at a time, until the potatoes are moistened. Marinate at room temperature for at least 1 hour.

Add the green onions, celery, bell peppers, onion, parsley, salt, black pepper, and hot-pepper sauce and toss well to combine.

BIG EASY SPINACH AND ROASTED PEPPER SALAD

MAKES 6 SERVINGS

This recipe is appropriately named because it is simple to prepare and the perfect salad to take along on a picnic. Okra Croutons (page 136) are delicious with this salad.

1	jar (19 ounces) roasted red bell peppers, drained and oil reserved
1	pound baby spinach leaves
12	cherry tomatoes, halved
1	small purple onion, peeled and thinly sliced
¼	cup balsamic vinegar
1	teaspoon salt
1	teaspoon freshly ground black pepper
⅛	teaspoon cayenne pepper
½	cup chopped pecans, toasted

Slice the roasted peppers into thin strips. Combine the peppers, spinach, tomatoes, and onion in a large bowl.

Combine the vinegar, salt, black pepper, and cayenne pepper with the reserved oil from the roasted peppers in a measuring cup and pour it over the salad. Toss gently to combine. Sprinkle the pecans over the salad.

BAYOU BOIL

MAKES 8 SERVINGS

Here's a vegetarian version of the classic Louisiana method of boiling a huge pot of seafood and vegetables and dumping the contents on a newspaper-covered table for all to feast on. It's a great way to serve a crowd outdoors in the summertime!

- 2 pounds new potatoes, halved
- 6 ounces green peanuts, unshelled
- 8 ribs celery
- 4 large green or red bell peppers, seeded, ribs removed, and quartered
- 2 large yellow onions, peeled and quartered
- 1 lemon, quartered
- 2 cloves garlic, peeled
- 2 bay leaves
- 2 tablespoons Cajun Spice Mix (page 123) or prepared Cajun spice mix
- 8 ears corn, shucked, silks removed, and cut in half
- 2 pounds broccoli, ends trimmed and cut into stems with the florets attached
- 3 pounds soy Italian link sausage

Combine the potatoes, peanuts, celery, bell peppers, onions, lemon, garlic, bay leaves, and Cajun Spice Mix in a straining basket in a large stock pot. Cover the ingredients with water. Bring the mixture to a boil over high heat. Cook for 5 minutes.

Layer the corn and broccoli on top of the other ingredients. Bring the mixture back to a boil. Cook for 10 to 15 minutes. Add the sausage on top of the corn and broccoli. Cover and return to a boil.

Remove the pot from the heat. The potatoes should be tender when pierced with a fork. Let the ingredients cool, covered, for 5 to 10 minutes. Remove the straining basket or carefully strain off all of the water and discard it. Remove and discard the bay leaves and lemon. Serve by dumping the boiled ingredients on a brown paper- or newspaper-covered table outside, or serve indoors in large, individual bowls.

Cooking Tip: If you don't have a pot that is large enough to boil all the vegetables in, prepare the recipe in batches, or divide it in half and prepare a smaller amount.

LOUISIANA LENTIL STEW

MAKES 6 SERVINGS

I've fallen in love with lentils and the special way they infuse a dish with rich flavor and body. This stew has a hearty, chili-like consistency.

1	tablespoon olive oil
1	medium yellow onion, peeled and chopped
2	cloves garlic, peeled and minced
1½	cups water
2	bay leaves
1	teaspoon salt
½	cup brown lentils, picked over and rinsed
1	can (20 ounces) peeled whole tomatoes, crushed
⅓	cup dry red wine
3	tablespoons tomato paste
1	teaspoon sugar
1	teaspoon freshly ground black pepper
1	teaspoon dried basil
1	teaspoon dried oregano
½	teaspoon dried thyme
⅛	teaspoon cayenne pepper
1	large zucchini, chopped

Heat the oil in a large pot over medium-high heat. Add the onion and garlic and sauté for 10 minutes, or until the onion is golden. Add the water, bay leaves, and salt.

Increase the heat to high and bring the mixture to a boil. Add the lentils and boil for 2 to 3 minutes. Reduce the heat to low and simmer for 30 minutes, stirring occasionally.

Stir in the tomatoes (with juice), wine, tomato paste, sugar, black pepper, basil, oregano, thyme, and cayenne pepper. Increase the heat to high and bring to a boil. Reduce the heat to low and simmer for 10 minutes. Stir in the zucchini and simmer for an additional 15 minutes. Remove and discard the bay leaves before serving.

OKRA GUMBO

Okra has as many fans as it does detractors. It can be served a number of ways, from fried to fritters to pickles and beyond. In soups and stews, okra is used as a thickener. It has also been used as a source of cooking oil. Ripe okra seeds have even been roasted, ground, and brewed as a substitute for coffee. This vegetarian version of an old Creole favorite retains the flavors of the original.

¼ cup olive oil

¼ cup (½ stick) unsalted butter

2 large yellow onions, peeled and chopped

3 cloves garlic, peeled and minced

2 green bell peppers, seeded, ribs removed, and chopped

1 jalapeño chile pepper, chopped (wear plastic gloves when handling)

3 pounds okra, tips and ends removed and sliced into rounds

4 cans (20 ounces) peeled whole tomatoes, crushed

1 small bunch flat-leaf parsley, chopped, or 2 tablespoons dried

3 tablespoons ketchup

2 tablespoons Caribbean hot sauce, such as Pickapeppa, or Vegetarian Worcestershire Sauce (page 255)

2 teaspoons sweet ground paprika

2 teaspoons freshly ground black pepper

2 teaspoons salt

1 tablespoon sugar

Juice of ½ lemon

2 cups uncooked long-grain white rice

Heat the oil and butter in a large, heavy nonstick pot over medium-high heat. Add the onions, garlic, bell peppers, and chile pepper. Sauté for 10 minutes, or until the onion is golden and the vegetables are tender. Remove to a bowl with a slotted spoon and set aside.

Add the okra to the pot and simmer for 10 minutes, stirring often. Return the vegetable mixture to the pot. Stir in the tomatoes (with juice), parsley, ketchup, hot sauce or Worcestershire sauce, paprika, black pepper, salt, and sugar. Cover and simmer for 30 to 40 minutes, stirring occasionally to keep the ingredients from sticking. Sprinkle with the lemon juice.

Meanwhile, prepare the rice according to package directions. Serve the gumbo over the rice.

Cooking Tip: Use green or red okra pods, no more than 2 to 3 inches long, to ensure tenderness. To avoid a gummy texture, don't slice the okra pods until you're ready to use them.

LOUISIANA-STYLE BLACK-EYED PEA SOUP WITH OKRA CROUTONS

MAKES 8 SERVINGS

Black-eyed peas—or cowpeas, as they were traditionally called—and okra are African imports to the American table. This tasty soup's perfect companion is a big slice of steaming hot cornbread.

OKRA CROUTONS

2   pounds okra, thinly sliced
1   cup cornmeal
1   teaspoon salt
½   teaspoon ground cumin
¼   teaspoon cayenne pepper

LOUISIANA-STYLE BLACK-EYED PEA SOUP

4   cups vegetable broth
2   cups water
2   tablespoons Vegetarian Worcestershire Sauce (page 255) or prepared vegetarian Worcestershire sauce
1   teaspoon salt
1   teaspoon freshly ground black pepper
2   bags (16 ounces each) frozen black-eyed peas
1   large yellow onion, peeled and chopped
1   medium green bell pepper, seeded, ribs removed, and chopped
1   medium red bell pepper, seeded, ribs removed, and chopped
2   ribs celery, chopped
2   bay leaves
4   green onions, trimmed and sliced

To prepare the Okra Croutons: Preheat the oven to 375 degrees. Rinse the okra in a colander. Drain and pat dry with paper towels.

Combine the okra, cornmeal, ½ teaspoon of the salt, cumin, and pepper in a zip-top plastic bag. Seal the bag and shake well.

Coat a baking sheet with olive oil cooking spray. Spread the okra in a single layer on the prepared baking sheet. Coat the okra with the cooking spray.

Bake for 10 minutes. Stir the okra and spray with the cooking spray again. Bake for an additional 15 minutes, or until crisp and golden brown. Sprinkle with the remaining ½ teaspoon salt.

To prepare the Louisiana-Style Black-Eyed Pea Soup: Meanwhile, combine the vegetable broth, water, Worcestershire sauce, salt, and black pepper in a large pot over high heat. Bring to a boil. Add the black-eyed peas, onion, bell peppers, celery, and bay leaves and cook for 8 to 10 minutes, or until the peas are tender. Remove and discard the bay leaves.

Mash half of the peas with a potato masher or immersion blender to thicken the soup. Ladle the soup into individual bowls and sprinkle with the green onions and the okra croutons.

Cooking Tip: Use green or red okra pods, no more than 2 to 3 inches long, to ensure tenderness. To avoid a gummy texture, don't slice the okra pods until you're ready to use them.

GUMBO Z'HERBES (GREEN GUMBO)

This vegetarian gumbo is served during the Lenten season, which begins the day after Fat Tuesday, following the Mardi Gras parties. Legend has it that the more variety of greens you put in this soup, the more friends you will make. I think it's because this gumbo is so good that people naturally fall in love with the cook!

3	ribs celery
2	mediums carrots, halved
1	medium yellow onion, peeled and quartered
1	medium green bell pepper, seeded, ribs removed, and quartered
2	cloves garlic, peeled
2	tablespoons olive oil
4	cups vegetable broth
1	can (20 ounces) peeled whole tomatoes, crushed
1	package (16 ounces) frozen chopped collard greens, thawed
1	package (16 ounces) frozen mustard greens, thawed
1	can (15 ounces) kidney beans, rinsed and drained
1	box (8 ounces) frozen chopped spinach, thawed
1	small head green cabbage, chopped
1	package (16 ounces) fresh or frozen okra, chopped
1	bunch flat-leaf parsley, finely chopped
2	tablespoons dried parsley
2	bay leaves
1	tablespoon dried oregano
1	teaspoon dried thyme
1	teaspoon salt
1	teaspoon freshly ground black pepper
½	teaspoon sugar
⅛	teaspoon cayenne pepper
2	cups uncooked long-grain white rice
4	green onions, trimmed and chopped

Place the celery, carrots, onion, bell pepper, and garlic in a food processor. Working in batches, pulse to chop the vegetables but do not puree.

Heat the oil in a large pot over medium-high heat. Add the onion mixture and sauté for 10 minutes, stirring occasionally, or until the vegetables are tender. Stir in the vegetable broth, tomatoes (with juice), collard greens, mustard greens, beans, spinach, cabbage, okra, parsley, bay leaves, oregano, thyme, salt, black pepper, sugar, and cayenne pepper. Reduce the heat to medium-low, cover and cook for 20 to 30 minutes, stirring occasionally. Remove and discard the bay leaves.

Meanwhile, prepare the rice according to package directions. Serve the gumbo over the rice and sprinkle with the green onions.

Cooking Tip: Use green or red okra pods, no more than 2 to 3 inches long, to ensure tenderness. To avoid a gummy texture, don't slice the okra pods until you're ready to use them.

CREOLE EGGS

This flavorful dish has two different sauces—a spicy tomato sauce and a creamy white sauce—that are layered with the hard-cooked eggs. You whip up the sauces in the time it takes the eggs to cook. Serve this recipe as a brunch dish or as a dinner meal with crowd-pleasing results!

EGGS

10	eggs
½	teaspoon salt
½	teaspoon freshly ground black pepper
½	teaspoon sweet ground paprika

TOMATO SAUCE

1	tablespoon olive oil
1	tablespoon butter
2	ribs celery, chopped
1	medium yellow onion, finely chopped
1	can (10 ounces) diced tomatoes with green chilies
½	teaspoon salt
½	teaspoon freshly ground black pepper
½	teaspoon sweet ground paprika
½	teaspoon sugar

CREAM SAUCE

2	tablespoons butter
2	tablespoons whole wheat or all-purpose flour
1	cup plain soy milk, at room temperature
1	teaspoon dried tarragon
½	teaspoon salt
½	teaspoon freshly ground black pepper

ASSEMBLY

2	cups (8 ounces) shredded mild Cheddar cheese
1½	cups fresh or dried bread crumbs
2	tablespoons butter

To prepare the eggs: Place the eggs in a large, heavy saucepan in a single layer. Cover with cold water. Partially cover the saucepan with a lid and place over high heat. Bring the eggs to a full boil. Reduce the heat to low, cover, and cook for 30 seconds. Remove the pan from the heat and keep covered. Allow the eggs to stand in the hot water for 15 minutes. Drain the hot water and fill the pan with cold water. Allow the eggs to stand for an additional 5 minutes.

Peel the eggs and slice each lengthwise into 3 thick pieces. Sprinkle the eggs with the salt, pepper, and paprika. Set the eggs aside.

To prepare the tomato sauce: Meanwhile, heat the oil and butter in a medium skillet over medium-high heat. Add the celery and onion and sauté for 7 minutes, or until the vegetables soften. Add the tomatoes (with juice), salt, pepper, paprika, and sugar. Cook for 8 to 10 minutes, or until the sauce begins to thicken. Remove from the heat.

To prepare the cream sauce: Melt the butter in a small skillet over medium-low heat. Add the flour and cook for 3 to 5 minutes, stirring constantly, until the mixture is smooth. Stir in the soy milk, tarragon, salt, and pepper. Increase the heat to high and bring to a boil. Cook for 3 to 5 minutes, stirring constantly, or until the mixture thickens. Remove the sauce from the heat.

To assemble: Preheat the oven to 350 degrees.

Cover the bottom of a 3-quart casserole dish with one-quarter of the tomato sauce. Add one-quarter of the eggs. Cover the eggs with one-quarter of the cream sauce, then another layer of the tomato sauce. The sauces will run together. Add one-quarter of the cheese. Repeat layering to use the remaining ingredients, topping the dish with the bread crumbs and any remaining cheese. Dot the butter over the top of the crumbs.

Bake for 20 minutes, or until the top is brown and begins to bubble.

ETHNIC-STYLE JAMBALAYA

MAKES 6 SERVINGS

This recipe is so similar to West African Jollof rice, it's probably an import that has been adapted for Creole kitchens. Some people think that jambalaya got its name from a corruption of jambon, *the French word for ham, which used to be one of the main ingredients. This ethnic-style version uses chicken-flavored seitan, a meat substitute that is made out of wheat gluten, and a Italian link sausage made out of soy, with delicious results.*

2	tablespoons olive oil
2	tablespoons butter
8	ounces chicken-flavored seitan, drained and sliced into ½-inch-thick pieces
12	ounces soy Italian link sausage, sliced into ½-inch-thick pieces
3	ribs celery, chopped
2	medium green bell peppers, seeded, ribs removed, and chopped
2	cloves garlic, peeled and minced
1	large yellow onion, peeled and chopped
2	cups uncooked long-grain white rice
¾	cup tomato sauce
2	tablespoons Cajun Spice Mix (page 123) or prepared Cajun seasoning
2	bay leaves
1	teaspoon salt
3	cups vegetable broth

Heat the oil and butter in a large, heavy-bottomed skillet over medium heat. Add the seitan and soy sausage and cook for 3 minutes, or until lightly browned.

Remove the seitan and sausage from the pan and set aside. Add the celery, bell peppers, garlic, and onion to the pan. Sauté for 8 minutes, or until tender. Stir in the rice, tomato sauce, Cajun Spice Mix, bay leaves, and salt. Simmer for 6 minutes, stirring constantly. Stir in the vegetable broth. Increase the heat to high and bring the mixture to a boil, stirring occasionally. Reduce the heat to low, cover, and simmer for 20 minutes, or until the rice is tender. Add the reserved seitan and sausage to the skillet and stir to combine. Cover the skillet, remove from the heat, and let stand for 5 minutes. Remove and discard the bay leaves before serving.

PORTOBELLO MUFFULETTA

MAKES 4 SERVINGS

This New Orleans favorite is taken to new heights with the tasty addition of pan-seared portobello mushrooms.

2	portobello mushrooms (about 8 ounces each), stems removed
2	tablespoons olive oil
1	teaspoon salt
1	teaspoon freshly ground black pepper
1	loaf round Italian bread, sliced in half horizontally
½	cup Olive Salad (page 125)
½	pound mild, white cheese (such as Havarti, Swiss, or Monterey Jack), thinly sliced
½	pound provolone cheese, thinly sliced
¼	pound mozzarella cheese, thinly sliced

Slice the mushroom caps at an angle into ½-inch-thick pieces. Brush with 1 tablespoon of the oil.

Coat the bottom of a heavy pan or cast-iron skillet with the remaining 1 tablespoon oil and place over high heat until hot but not smoking. Add the mushroom slices and sear for 4 to 5 minutes. Turn the slices over and sear on the other side for 3 to 4 minutes, or until browned. Remove to a plate and sprinkle with the salt and pepper.

Tear out some of the bread from the center of the bottom half. Place in a zip-top plastic bag and freeze for another use. Brush the top and bottom parts of the bread generously with the oil from the Olive Salad. Place the mushrooms in the hollowed-out bread half. Layer the white cheese, provolone, and mozzarella on top of the mushrooms, then add a layer of the Olive Salad.

Place the top half of the bread on the Olive Salad. Press down on the top of the sandwich firmly to mingle the ingredients. Cut into 4 wedges.

EGGPLANT SOUFFLÉ

This elegant dish is like a jazz composition: Each ingredient plays a solo, but all of them harmonize together beautifully.

2	tablespoons butter
2	tablespoons olive oil
2	ribs celery, chopped
1	large yellow onion, peeled and chopped
2	cloves garlic, peeled and minced
6	sprigs parsley, chopped
4	leaves fresh basil, torn
1	tablespoon whole wheat or all-purpose flour
1	tablespoon dried thyme
1	teaspoon salt
1	teaspoon freshly ground black pepper
⅛	teaspoon cayenne pepper
¾	cup plain soy milk
1	large (about 1½ pounds) eggplant, peeled and chopped
2	cups (8 ounces) shredded Monterey Jack cheese
½	cup fresh or dried bread crumbs
3	eggs, separated
½	teaspoon cream of tartar

Preheat the oven to 350 degrees. Coat a 1½-quart baking pan with cooking spray.

Heat the butter and oil in a large skillet over medium-high heat. Add the celery, onion, and garlic. Sauté for 10 minutes, or until tender. Sprinkle the parsley, basil, flour, thyme, salt, black pepper, and cayenne pepper over the vegetables. Stir until well-combined. Stir in the soy milk and eggplant. Reduce the heat to low and cook, stirring occasionally, for 10 minutes, or until the eggplant is tender.

Remove the eggplant mixture to a large bowl. Add the cheese, bread crumbs, and egg yolks. Stir until well-combined.

Place the egg whites and cream of tartar in a stainless steel or glass bowl. With an electric mixer on high speed, beat the egg whites until stiff peaks form. Fold the egg whites, a few tablespoons at a time, into the eggplant mixture. Pour the eggplant mixture into the prepared baking pan.

Bake for 40 to 45 minutes, or until the soufflé is puffy and golden brown. Allow the soufflé to sit for 5 minutes before serving.

VEGETABLE-STUFFED MIRLITONS

MAKES 4 SERVINGS

Mirlitons are a member of the gourd family and taste like a cross between an apple and a cucumber. They are called mirlitons in the Louisiana area and chayote in Texas, parts of the Southwest, and Mexico. This dish is delicious by any name.

2	tablespoons butter, softened
1	quart cold water
4	medium (about 8 ounces each) mirlitons, halved lengthwise
1	teaspoon salt
1	tablespoon olive oil
1	cup baby spinach leaves or 1 box (10 ounces) frozen chopped spinach, thawed and squeezed dry
4	ounces button mushrooms, sliced
2	cloves garlic, peeled and minced
1½	cups toasted bread crumbs
½	cup freshly grated Parmesan cheese
¼	cup vegetable broth
1	egg, beaten
1	teaspoon salt
1	teaspoon freshly ground black pepper
⅛	teaspoon cayenne pepper

Preheat the oven to 350 degrees. Lightly grease a 2-quart square baking dish with 1 tablespoon of the butter.

Place the water, mirlitons, and salt in a large pot over high heat. The water should just cover the mirlitons; add more, if needed. Bring the ingredients to a boil. Reduce the heat to low, cover, and simmer for 12 minutes, or until the mirlitons are tender. Remove from the heat. Allow the ingredients to cool. Drain and discard the water.

When the mirlitons are cool enough to handle, scoop out the seeds and discard. Scoop out the pulp, leaving a ¼-inch shell. Turn the shells over to drain any excess liquid. Press the pulp between two paper towels to absorb excess liquid. Chop the pulp and set aside.

Heat the oil and the remaining 1 tablespoon butter in a large skillet over medium-high heat. Add the spinach, mushrooms, and garlic. Sauté for 10 minutes, or until the vegetables are tender. Stir in the mirliton pulp, bread crumbs, ¼ cup of the cheese, the vegetable broth, egg, salt, black pepper, and cayenne pepper. Reduce the heat to low and cook for 7 minutes to blend the flavors.

Place the mirliton shells in the prepared baking dish. Mound the stuffing mixture in the shells. Cover with a piece of foil.

Bake for 20 minutes. Remove the foil and sprinkle the mirlitons with the remaining ¼ cup cheese. Bake for 3 to 5 minutes, or until the cheese melts.

Cooking Tip: Choose mirlitons that have firm, smooth skin with slight ridges running from stem to end. The skin should be free of blemishes and moldy spots.

OKRA AND CORN *ÉTOUFFÉE*

MAKES 6 SERVINGS

Étouffée is a French term meaning to smother or suffocate and l'étouffée refers to the method of cooking food in a small amount of liquid, tightly covered, over low heat. In this recipe, the okra is smothered by a spicy tomato sauce. Bell pepper, onions, and celery are a frequent combination in Creole dishes. These three ingredients reflect the French influence, while the corn, tomatoes, and chile peppers are the African touch.

2	tablespoons olive oil
1	tablespoon butter
2	ribs celery, chopped
1	large yellow onion, peeled and chopped
1	medium green bell pepper, seeded, ribs removed, and chopped
1	jalapeño chile pepper, chopped (wear plastic gloves when handling)
3	cups (about 2 pounds) okra, sliced
1½	cups fresh or frozen and thawed corn kernels
1	can (20 ounces) peeled whole tomatoes, crushed
1	tablespoon tomato paste
1	tablespoon Cajun Spice Mix (page 123) or prepared Cajun seasoning
½	teaspoon sugar
½	cup vegetable broth
1½	cups uncooked long-grain white rice

Heat the oil and butter in a large skillet over medium-high heat. Add the celery, onion, bell pepper, and chile pepper. Sauté for 10 minutes, or until the vegetables are tender. Add the okra and corn and sauté for 7 minutes. Add the tomatoes (with juice), tomato paste, Cajun Spice Mix, and sugar and sauté for 5 minutes.

Stir in the vegetable broth and bring to a boil. Reduce the heat to low, cover, and simmer for 15 minutes, stirring occasionally.

Meanwhile, prepare the rice according to package directions. Serve the étoufée over the rice in individual bowls.

Cooking Tip: Use green or red okra pods, 2 to 3 inches long, to insure tenderness. To avoid a gummy texture, don't slice the okra pods until you're ready to use them.

DIRTY RICE

Dirty rice is a traditional side dish that I've promoted to main-dish status with the addition of soy sausage and chicken-flavored seitan, two vegetarian meat substitutes. Add a salad and a hot, buttery slice of cornbread, and you'll have a memorable meal, I guarantee!

2	cups uncooked long-grain white rice
4¼	cups vegetable broth
1	bunch green onions, trimmed and chopped
2	bay leaves
2	tablespoons olive oil
2	tablespoons butter
2	ribs celery, chopped
1	large yellow onion, peeled and chopped
1	small green bell pepper, seeded, ribs removed, and chopped
2	cloves garlic, peeled and minced
8	ounces soy sausage patties, chopped
8	ounces chicken-flavored seitan, drained and chopped
2	ounces shiitake mushrooms, chopped
1	tablespoon Cajun Spice Mix (page 123) or prepared Cajun seasoning

Place the rice in a colander and rinse under cold, running water several times until the water runs clear. Place the rice, 4 cups of the vegetable broth, green onions, and bay leaves in a large pot over high heat. Bring the rice to a rolling boil. Reduce the heat to low, cover, and simmer for 20 minutes. Do not overcook.

Heat the oil and butter in a large skillet over medium-high heat. Add the celery, onion, bell pepper, and garlic. Sauté for 10 minutes, or until the vegetables soften. Add the soy sausage, seitan, mushrooms, the remaining ¼ cup vegetable broth, and the Cajun Spice Mix. Cook, stirring occasionally, for 10 minutes to blend the flavors.

Add the rice to the pan and mix well. Reduce the heat to low and simmer for 7 minutes, stirring occasionally, to blend the flavors.

GARLIC MASHED POTATOES WITH BROCCOLI COULIS

MAKES 6 SERVINGS

This dish is what I call Creole comfort food. A coulis is a puree of fruit or vegetables used as a sauce. Wine or broth is added to thin the coulis, but not so much as to alter the intense flavor. And there's nothing like the creamy taste of mashed potatoes, especially when they've been combined with garlic and the soft tofu. Serve with some crusty bread for a wonderful meal.

GARLIC MASHED POTATOES

4½	pounds boiling potatoes, peeled and sliced
¼	cup + 2 tablespoons butter, softened
4	ounces cream cheese, softened
4	ounces soft, silken tofu, drained
½	cup heavy cream
2	cloves garlic, peeled and minced
2	teaspoons salt
1	teaspoon ground white pepper

BROCCOLI COULIS

1¼	pounds broccoli, stems peeled and chopped, and florets separated
½	bunch green onions, trimmed and chopped
1	bay leaf
1	teaspoon salt
2	tablespoons butter
1	teaspoon salt
½	teaspoon ground white pepper
⅛	teaspoon freshly grated nutmeg
2	teaspoons freshly squeezed lemon juice
2	tablespoons heavy whipping cream

To prepare the Garlic Mashed Potatoes: Place the potatoes into a large pot over high heat. Cover with water and bring to a boil. Boil for 15 to 20 minutes, or until the potatoes are tender when pierced with a fork. Drain the water and discard.

Place the potatoes in a large bowl. Add the butter and with an electric mixer on medium speed, beat until the potatoes are creamy. Reduce the speed to low and add the cream cheese, tofu, cream, garlic, salt, and pepper. Blend until the potatoes are fluffy.

To prepare the Broccoli Coulis: Meanwhile, bring 2 quarts of water to a boil in a large saucepan over medium-high heat. Add the broccoli, green onions, bay leaf, and salt. Cook for 6 minutes, or until the broccoli stems are tender. Remove with a slotted spoon to a food processor or blender. Remove and discard the bay leaf and reserve the cooking water. Add the butter, salt, pepper, nutmeg, and lemon juice to the food processor. Process to puree for 1 minute, leaving some texture to the sauce. Add a little of the reserved cooking liquid, if needed, to loosen the mixture to a sauce consistency. Stir in the cream. Serve over the potatoes.

CREOLE RICE CAKES WITH SPICY TOMATO SAUCE

MAKES 6 SERVINGS

Creole dishes are traditionally spicy and often contain tomatoes, onions, and peppers. This delicious dish appears to be complicated but is really fairly simple to prepare and well worth the effort. The rice cakes remind me of traditional African fu fu *in texture, but these cakes are a little firmer.*

SPICY TOMATO SAUCE

2	tablespoons olive oil
½	stick butter
2	cloves garlic, peeled and minced
1	large yellow onion, peeled and chopped
2	ribs celery, chopped
1	green bell pepper, seeded, ribs removed, and chopped
1	small zucchini, chopped
1	tablespoon dried oregano
1	teaspoon ground cumin
1	teaspoon salt
1	teaspoon sugar
¼	teaspoon freshly grated nutmeg
3	cans (8 ounces each) tomato sauce
½	cup vegetable broth
2	tablespoons salsa
4	ounces shitake mushrooms, chopped

CREOLE RICE CAKES

4	large eggs
1½	cups uncooked long-grain white rice
1	cup oat bran
1	cup Spicy Tomato Sauce (recipe above)
1	teaspoon salt
8	sprigs parsley

To prepare the Spicy Tomato Sauce: Heat the oil and butter in a medium saucepan over medium-high heat. Add the garlic and onion and sauté for 10 minutes, or until golden. Add the celery, bell pepper, zucchini, oregano, cumin, salt, sugar, and nutmeg. Sauté for 10 minutes, or until tender. Stir in the tomato sauce, vegetable broth, and salsa and bring the mixture to a boil. Reduce the heat to low and simmer for 10 minutes, stirring occasionally. Remove 1 cup of the sauce and set aside to add to the rice cake mixture, removing any vegetables and returning them to the pan. Add the mushrooms to the pan and cook for 2 minutes.

To prepare the Creole Rice Cakes: Prepare the rice according to package directions. Cool completely. Preheat the oven to 350 degrees.

Beat the eggs in a large bowl until foamy. Add the rice, oat bran, reserved 1 cup Spicy Tomato Sauce, and salt. Mix well.

Grease a 12-cup muffin tin with shortening.

Evenly divide the rice mixture among the cups, filling the containers to the rim. Bake for 25 minutes, or until the rice cakes are dry to the touch. Cool the cakes slightly. Run a sharp knife around the edge of each cake to loosen them from the cups and place the cakes on individual serving plates.

Ladle the Spicy Tomato Sauce over the cakes. Garnish with the parsley sprigs.

CALAS

MAKES 24 *CALAS*

Calas *is the word for rice in many African dialects. African-American cooks sold these cinnamon-flavored snacks throughout the French Quarter in New Orleans in the late 1800s. This is a modern version of that old favorite.*

1½	cups uncooked long-grain white rice
1½	cups self-rising flour
½	cup granulated sugar
½	teaspoon salt
½	teaspoon ground cinnamon
½	teaspoon freshly grated nutmeg
3	large eggs, beaten
½	teaspoon vanilla extract
¼	cup whole vanilla-flavored soy milk
	Vegetable oil for frying
	Confectioners' sugar

Prepare the rice according to package directions. Set aside to cool.

Combine the flour, granulated sugar, salt, cinnamon, and nutmeg in a large bowl. With an electric mixer on medium speed, blend in the eggs, vanilla extract, and soy milk. Stir in the rice, mixing thoroughly. Shape the rice mixture into Ping-Pong-size balls.

Heat the oil in a deep, heavy skillet over high heat until hot but not smoking (375 degrees). Carefully add the rice balls and fry for 2 to 3 minutes, or until golden brown. Remove the balls from the oil with a slotted spoon to a paper towel–covered plate to drain. Dust the calas with confectioners' sugar.

CREOLE PRALINES

During slavery, African-American cooks sold this sugary confection on the streets of New Orleans. It's still a popular treat today.

2	cups chopped pecans
2	tablespoons butter, melted
¼	teaspoon salt
1½	cups packed brown sugar
1½	cups granulated sugar
1½	cups evaporated milk
1	teaspoon vanilla extract

Preheat the oven to 400 degrees.

Spread the pecans on a large baking sheet and place in the oven. Toast the nuts for 10 to 12 minutes, or until lightly browned. Toss the nuts with 1 tablespoon of the butter and the salt.

Combine the brown sugar, granulated sugar, and milk in a large saucepan over medium-high heat. Cook, stirring constantly, for 15 to 20 minutes, or until the mixture reaches 236 degrees on a candy thermometer. Remove the saucepan from the heat and set aside to cool to room temperature, undisturbed, for 5 minutes. Stir in the vanilla extract and pecans, mixing well for 2 to 3 minutes. Place heaping tablespoonfuls of the mixture about 2 inches apart on a piece of waxed paper. Allow the pralines to harden for 5 to 8 minutes. Store in an airtight container.

SOUTHERN VEGETARIAN RECIPES

Thanks to my father's career in the Air Force, my family traveled from one part of the United States to the other (and into parts of Canada), but I'm the only one of us who was born in the South. So even though I grew up all over the place, it's always felt right to me that I love Southern cooking and Southern hospitality so much.

Many traditions that we associate with "Southern hospitality" are similar to customs found in Africa. For example, it is unthinkable in Africa to allow a stranger to go away hungry. In many places the common greeting is "have you eaten today?"

Despite the horrible conditions that forced many Africans to America, that generosity of spirit traveled with them and became a way of life here.

African influence on the American South is also clearly visible in the cookbooks produced at the end of the eighteenth century. *The Virginia Housewife* by Mary Randolph, published in 1824, included three dishes containing the African staple okra, as well as a recipe including another important ingredient in African cooking, peanuts. Sarah Rutledge's cookbook *The Carolina Housewife*, published in 1847, used *benne*, or sesame seeds as they are most commonly known, as well as peanuts in her candy recipes, and was one of the first cookbook authors to include a recipe for Hopping John.

Although the creators of the recipes in these cookbooks were never properly credited, culinary research attributes the use of peppers, rice, black-eyed peas, peanuts, and okra to inventive African and African-American cooks. Such dishes have become staples on many Southern dinner tables.

The recipes in this chapter embrace both my Southern roots and my new love of vegetarian cooking. While some adjustments have been made to bypass the pork that's common in many traditional Southern dishes, the flavors, techniques, and that ever-popular cast-iron skillet are still vital to the recipes.

Y'all enjoy!

▪ BREADS AND DESSERTS ▪

SOUTHERN SEASONING

MAKES ABOUT ¾ CUP

Southern food has a definitive spice, smell, and taste. This seasoning mix contains spices that are used over and over again in the recipes in this chapter. Use it liberally!

  2½ tablespoons ground paprika
  1 tablespoon salt
  2 tablespoons garlic powder
  1 tablespoon freshly ground black pepper
  1 tablespoon onion powder
  1 tablespoon dried oregano
  1 tablespoon dried thyme
  2 teaspoons parsley
  2 teaspoons celery seed
  2 teaspoons cayenne pepper

Place all ingredients in an airtight container. Cover securely and shake to combine the ingredients. Store in a cool, dry place.

COLESLAW

MAKES 8 TO 10 SERVINGS

Coleslaw is a must for a barbecue or picnic in the South. I like this recipe because it's quick, easy, and delicious. You can prepare the vegetables in a food processor or buy packaged shredded cabbage and add the dressing.

  2 pounds shredded cabbage
  ½ small yellow onion, peeled and grated
  1 small carrot, grated
  ⅔ cup apple cider vinegar
  ¾ cup sour cream
  1 teaspoon sugar
  1 teaspoon salt
  1 teaspoon freshly ground black pepper

Combine all ingredients in a large bowl. Refrigerate for at least 1 hour before serving.

'CUEING SAUCE

MAKES ABOUT 4½ CUPS

We call cooking food on a grill 'cueing, which is short for barbecuing here in the South. This delightfully sweet and spicy sauce is perfect whether you're 'cueing indoors or out.

3	cups ketchup
2	cups water
¼	cup packed brown sugar
1	small yellow onion, peeled and finely chopped
12	cloves garlic, peeled and minced
1	jalapeño chile pepper, finely chopped (wear plastic gloves when handling)
3	tablespoons Vegetarian Worcestershire Sauce (page 255)
2	tablespoons molasses
1	tablespoon olive oil
	Juice of 1 lemon
1½	teaspoons stone-ground mustard

Combine all ingredients in a large, nonaluminum skillet over low heat. Cook for 50 minutes, stirring occasionally. If the sauce is too thick, add 2 to 3 tablespoons more water. Store in an airtight container for 1 to 2 weeks.

Cooking Tip: If you like, you can use 1 bottle (45 ounces) of barbecue sauce instead of the ketchup and water and add all the other ingredients to it. Simmer the sauce for 15 to 20 minutes, stirring occasionally.

FRIED GREEN TOMATO AND DILL PICKLE SALAD

MAKES 6 SERVINGS

I created this unusual salad by combining two ingredients that are uniquely Southern: fried green tomatoes and fried dill pickles. I love the fresh taste of the green tomatoes, the crunch of the fried pickles, and the tartness that the dressing brings to the salad.

FRIED TOMATOES AND PICKLES

1½	cups cornmeal
1½	cups whole wheat or all-purpose flour
1	tablespoon Southern Seasoning (page 160)
2	large eggs
1	cup plain soy milk
2	tablespoons hot-pepper sauce
4	large green tomatoes, cut into ½-inch-thick slices
1	jar (16 ounces) sliced dill pickles, drained and patted dry, with juice reserved
4	cups vegetable oil
1	teaspoon salt

SALAD

½	cup olive oil
1	pound salad greens, such as romaine, iceberg, spinach, or a mixture
1	small purple onion, peeled and thinly sliced

To prepare the fried tomatoes and pickles: Sift the cornmeal, flour, and seasoning mix into a large bowl.

Combine the eggs, soy milk, and hot-pepper sauce in a medium bowl. Dip the tomato slices into the egg mixture and shake off any excess liquid. Dredge in the cornmeal mixture and shake off any excess coating. Place on a plate.

Dip the pickles in the egg mixture and shake off any excess liquid. Dredge in the cornmeal mixture and shake off any excess coating. Place on another plate.

Heat $\frac{1}{2}$ cup of the vegetable oil in a large, heavy-bottomed skillet over medium heat. Working in batches, place the tomato slices in the skillet. Allow plenty of space between the slices in the skillet. Cook the tomatoes for 3 to 4 minutes, or until golden brown. Turn them over to brown the other side. Remove from the oil with a slotted spoon to a paper towel–covered plate to drain. Sprinkle with $\frac{1}{2}$ teaspoon of the salt.

Add the remaining $3\frac{1}{2}$ cups vegetable oil to the skillet. Heat the oil to 350 degrees, or until a cube of bread fries to a golden brown within 2 minutes. Working in batches, add the pickles to the skillet and fry for 2 minutes, or until brown and crisp. Remove from the oil with a slotted spoon to a paper towel–covered plate to drain. Sprinkle with the remaining $\frac{1}{2}$ teaspoon salt.

To prepare the salad: Measure 3 tablespoons of the reserved pickle juice into a small bowl. Whisk in the oil.

Place the greens and onion in a large bowl. Drizzle the pickle juice dressing over the top and toss gently to combine. Top the salad with the fried tomatoes and pickles.

SUMMER SQUASH SALAD
WITH SPICY MUSTARD VINAIGRETTE

MAKES 6 SERVINGS

The spiciness of the vinaigrette adds a new dimension to this classic recipe.

SPICY MUSTARD VINAIGRETTE

- ¼ cup red wine vinegar
- 2 tablespoons chopped fresh cilantro
- 2 cloves garlic, peeled and crushed
- 1 tablespoon soy sauce
- 2 teaspoons spicy prepared mustard
- ¼ teaspoon salt
- ¼ teaspoon freshly ground black pepper
- ¾ cup olive oil

SUMMER SQUASH SALAD

- 1 tablespoon olive oil
- 1 tablespoon butter
- 8 yellow squash, sliced crosswise into ⅛-inch-thick pieces
- 1 teaspoon salt
- 1 teaspoon freshly ground black pepper
- ¼ teaspoon sugar
- 2 tablespoons water
- 2 large tomatoes
- 1 large yellow onion, peeled and chopped
- 1 green bell pepper, seeded, ribs removed, and chopped
- 1 pound salad greens, such as romaine, iceberg, spinach, or a mixture
- 2 tablespoons chopped parsley

To prepare the Spicy Mustard Vinaigrette: Combine the vinegar, cilantro, garlic, soy sauce, mustard, salt, and pepper in a small bowl. Slowly whisk in the oil until the mixture thickens. Set aside ½ cup for the salad. Reserve the remainder for another use.

To prepare the Summer Squash Salad: Heat the oil and butter in a large skillet over medium heat. Add the squash, salt, black pepper, and sugar and stir to combine. Increase the heat to high and cook for 4 minutes, stirring occasionally. Reduce the heat to low, add the water, and cook for an additional 4 minutes, or until the squash is crisp but tender. Remove the skillet from the heat and allow the squash to cool.

Place the squash in a large bowl. Add the tomatoes, onion, bell pepper, and the reserved ½ cup vinaigrette. Mix well to combine the ingredients.

Place the greens on a serving platter. Top with the squash salad. Sprinkle with the parsley.

Cooking Tips: Choose small- to medium-size squash with either crook-shape or straight necks and bright, shiny yellow skin.

Store the remaining vinaigrette in an airtight container in the refrigerator. It will keep for up to 10 days.

NORTH CAROLINA COLLARD SOUP

MAKES 8 SERVINGS

My father, Howard Shelf, is from Winston-Salem, North Carolina, and my mother, Angeline, has a garden full of collard greens. These family facts made it easy for me to fall in love with this classic recipe. It's a hearty soup that's perfect for a winter supper.

2	tablespoons olive oil
2	tablespoons butter
2	ribs celery, chopped
1	large yellow onion, peeled and chopped
1	green or red bell pepper, seeded, ribs removed, and chopped
2	cloves garlic, minced
1	jalapeño chile pepper, chopped (wear plastic gloves when handling)
4	cups vegetable broth
2	tablespoons red wine vinegar
2	teaspoons salt
1	teaspoon freshly ground black pepper
½	teaspoon sugar
2	bay leaves
2	bunches (about 2 pounds) young, tender collard greens, stems removed and cut into strips, or 2 packages (16 ounces each) frozen chopped collard greens, thawed and squeezed dry
4	boiling or Yellow Finn potatoes, scrubbed and cubed
12	ounces soy Italian link sausage, cut into ½-inch-thick pieces
⅓	cup half-and-half, at room temperature

Heat the oil and butter in a large pot over medium-high heat. Add the celery, onion, bell pepper, garlic, and chile pepper. Sauté for 7 to 10 minutes, or until the vegetables soften.

Add the vegetable broth, 1 tablespoon of the vinegar, the salt, black pepper, sugar, and bay leaves to the pot. Bring the mixture to a boil. Reduce the heat to low, cover, and simmer for 15 minutes to blend the flavors.

Increase the heat to high. Add the greens and potatoes to the pot. Stir the ingredients with a long-handled spoon, pushing them down into the broth to keep them immersed in the liquid. Reduce the heat to low, cover, and cook for 45 to 50 minutes, stirring occasionally.

Stir the sausage, half-and-half, and the remaining 1 tablespoon vinegar into the soup. Cover and cook for 10 minutes, or until the greens are tender. Remove and discard the bay leaves before serving.

SLAVES' QUARTERS VEGETABLE SOUP

MAKES 8 TO 10 SERVINGS

I've heard the song "Hambone, hambone where you been? Round the world and back again!" since I was young. I didn't realize the song was referring to the practice in the slaves' quarters of sharing a hambone to flavor a pot of beans, greens, or soup. The joke was that by the time the hambone made its way back to its original owner, there wasn't much of it left. I think that well-traveled hambone was more for looks than for actual flavor. This delicious soup uses the essence of the vegetables themselves to thicken and flavor it. No hambone is needed!

2	tablespoons olive oil
2	tablespoons butter
2	large yellow onions, peeled and chopped
1	bunch green onions, trimmed and chopped
4	ribs celery, chopped
3	cloves garlic, peeled and chopped
1	green or red bell pepper, seeded, ribs removed, and chopped
1	jalapeño chile pepper, chopped (wear plastic gloves when handling)
4	sprigs parsley, chopped
2	tablespoons Southern Seasoning (page 160)
3	medium tomatoes, diced, or 2 cans (14 ounces each) diced tomatoes
3	large baking potatoes, such as Idaho, Russet, or Irish, scrubbed and chopped
2	boiling potatoes, such as Yukon Gold, wax, or fingerling, scrubbed and sliced
2	medium carrots, scrubbed and chopped
1	cup fresh or frozen and thawed green beans
1	cup fresh or frozen and thawed corn kernels
1	cup chopped fresh or frozen and thawed okra
2	small turnips, scrubbed and chopped (optional)
1	cup chopped cabbage (optional)
3	quarts vegetable broth or water
1	teaspoon sugar
	Salt (optional)
	Freshly ground black pepper (optional)

Heat the oil and butter in a large pot over low heat. Add the yellow onions and green onions and cook for 10 minutes, stirring occasionally. Add the celery, garlic, bell pepper, chile pepper, parsley, and Southern Seasoning. Cook for 7 minutes, stirring occasionally. Add the tomatoes (with juice), baking potatoes, boiling potatoes, carrots, green beans, corn, and okra to the pot. Cook for 5 minutes, stirring occasionally. Add the turnips and cabbage, if desired.

Add the vegetable broth or water and the sugar. Reduce the heat to medium-low and cook for 30 to 40 minutes, stirring occasionally. Some of the baking potatoes will start to break apart. Gently mash the potatoes against the side of the pot and stir them back into the broth to help thicken the soup. Taste and season with salt and black pepper, if desired.

BARBECUED BEANS

MAKES 6 SERVINGS

This is an easy recipe for beans that requires little time to prepare but has a lot of flavor.

    2   cans (15 ounces each) pinto beans, black-eyed peas, or kidney beans
    1   cup prepared barbecue sauce or 'Cueing Sauce (page 161)

Place the beans and sauce in a medium saucepan over medium heat. Bring to a boil. Reduce the heat to low and simmer for 10 minutes, stirring occasionally.

ETHNIC-STYLE BARBECUE

MAKES 6 SERVINGS

Seitan, which is compressed wheat gluten, has a dense texture and is a flavorful substitute for meat. I've fooled several die-hard Texas beef lovers with this recipe. It's juicy and tender and makes a wonderful main-dish meal or a delicious barbecue sandwich.

    2   pounds beef-flavored seitan, drained, patted dry, and cut into
        ½-inch pieces
    1   teaspoon salt
    1   teaspoon freshly ground black pepper
    1   teaspoon hot-pepper sauce
    ⅛   teaspoon cayenne pepper
    2   tablespoons butter
    1   cup 'Cueing Sauce (page 161) or prepared barbecue sauce

Place the seitan in a large bowl and sprinkle with the salt, black pepper, hot-pepper sauce, and cayenne pepper. Toss to coat.

Melt the butter in a medium saucepan over medium-high heat. Add the seitan and sauté for 2 minutes. Stir in the barbecue sauce. Reduce the heat to low and cook for 20 minutes, stirring occasionally.

HOPPING JOHN

I've read a number of stories about how this bean-and-rice dish got its name from someone's mispronunciation of the name bahatta-kachang, *which is from a West African dialect; to the New Year's tradition of eating black-eyed peas but not letting the children have a serving until they hop around the table; to a one-legged waiter named John who supposedly served this dish at a Southern restaurant. No matter how this fabulous dish got its name, I can't think of a better way to start off a new year!*

2	tablespoons olive oil
1	tablespoon butter
1	yellow onion, peeled and chopped
2	cloves garlic, peeled and minced
2	ribs celery, chopped
1	small green bell pepper, seeded, ribs removed, and chopped
1	can (15 ounces) peeled whole tomatoes, drained
3	bay leaves
2	teaspoons salt
1	teaspoon freshly ground black pepper
1	teaspoon sugar
½	teaspoon dried thyme
½	teaspoon ground allspice
½	teaspoon cayenne pepper
2	cups fresh or frozen black-eyed peas
4	cups vegetable broth or water
1	cup uncooked long-grain white rice

Heat the oil and butter in a large pot over medium-high heat. Add the onion and sauté for 10 minutes, stirring occasionally. Add the garlic, celery, bell pepper, tomatoes, bay leaves, salt, black pepper, sugar, thyme, allspice, and cayenne pepper. Sauté for 5 minutes, stirring occasionally.

Stir the peas and vegetable broth or water into the pot. Bring to a boil. Reduce the heat to low, partially cover, and simmer for 1 hour, stirring occasionally. Add the rice, cover the pot tightly, and cook for 20 minutes, or until the peas and rice are tender.

CHEESE GRITS

Grits are a popular dish in the South and enjoyed by folks of all nationalities. The dish was a staple in my childhood. This version incorporates cheese and soy milk and is delicious as a main dish accompanied by a fruit salad and a crusty loaf of buttered bread.

¾	cup butter
4	cups water
1	teaspoon salt
1	cup hominy grits (not quick-cooking)
1	teaspoon garlic powder
2	cups (8 ounces) shredded mild Cheddar cheese
1	egg, at room temperature
¾	cup plain soy milk, at room temperature

Preheat the oven to 350 degrees. Grease a 2-quart baking dish with ¼ cup of the butter. Bring the water and salt to a boil in a large saucepan over high heat. Slowly stir in the grits. Cook for 3 minutes, stirring constantly. Remove the pan from the heat and stir in the remaining ½ cup butter, the garlic powder, and the cheese. Mix well.

Place the egg and soy milk in a small bowl. Mix well. Add the egg mixture to the grits mixture, stirring until well-combined. Pour the grits into the prepared casserole.

Bake for 1 hour, or until the casserole is firm.

MACARONI AND CHEESE

James Hemings, Thomas Jefferson's slave chef, learned how to make macaroni and cheese in France and often prepared it for Jefferson's guests. The tofu in this recipe makes it especially creamy and nutritious.

1	pound elbow macaroni
¼	cup + 1 tablespoon butter
¼	cup whole wheat or all-purpose flour
2½	cups plain soy milk, at room temperature
4	ounces Velveeta cheese, cubed
1	cup (4 ounces) shredded sharp Cheddar cheese
2	ounces soft, silken tofu, drained
1	teaspoon salt
1	teaspoon freshly ground black pepper
⅛	teaspoon cayenne pepper
⅛	teaspoon freshly grated nutmeg
1	egg, lightly beaten
1	cup (4 ounces) freshly grated Parmesan cheese
1	teaspoon ground paprika

Preheat the oven to 350 degrees. Coat an 11 × 7 inch baking dish with cooking spray.

Prepare the macaroni according to package directions. Drain and place in the prepared baking dish. Add 1 tablespoon of the butter and toss to coat.

Melt the remaining 4 tablespoons butter in a small saucepan over medium heat. Whisk in the flour and cook for 1 to 2 minutes, stirring constantly. Increase the heat to high and whisk in the soy milk, stirring constantly. Bring the mixture to a boil, stirring until the sauce is smooth and thick. Reduce the heat to low. Add the Velveeta, Cheddar, and tofu. Cook, stirring, for 6 to 8 minutes, or until the cheese and tofu blend smoothly. Stir in the salt, black pepper, cayenne pepper, and nutmeg. Pour the sauce mixture over the cooked pasta and mix well. Stir in the egg and Parmesan. Sprinkle with the paprika.

Bake for 35 to 40 minutes, or until the casserole is bubbling and the top begins to brown.

CHICKEN-FRIED STEAK SEITAN WITH CREAM GRAVY

MAKES 6 TO 8 SERVINGS

I've adapted the recipe for chicken-fried steak to my new ethnic vegetarian lifestyle by substituting seitan. Serve this dish with a side of mashed potatoes and a salad, and you'll have a real Texas-style dinner.

CHICKEN-FRIED STEAK SEITAN

- 1 cup whole wheat pastry flour
- 3 tablespoons arrowroot flour
- 1 teaspoon salt
- ¼ teaspoon freshly ground black pepper
- ¼ teaspoon cayenne pepper
- ½ teaspoon dried thyme
- ½ teaspoon onion powder
- ½ teaspoon garlic powder
- ¼ teaspoon celery seeds
- 1½ cups water
- ½ cup vegetable oil
- 2 pounds beef-flavored seitan, drained, patted dry, and cut into 6 to 8 cutlets

CREAM GRAVY

- 3 tablespoons whole wheat pastry flour
- 2 teaspoons Southern Seasoning (page 160)
- ½ cup water, at room temperature
- ½ cup plain soy milk, at room temperature
- 1 tablespoon Vegetarian Worcestershire Sauce (page 255)

To prepare the Chicken-Fried Steak Seitan: Place the whole wheat flour, arrowroot flour, salt, black pepper, cayenne pepper, thyme, onion powder, garlic powder, and celery seeds in a large bowl. Add the water and stir to combine. Some lumps may remain. Refrigerate the batter for 10 minutes.

Heat the oil in a large, deep skillet over medium-high heat until hot but not smoking. Dredge the seitan in the batter and shake off any excess batter. Working in batches, place the seitan in the skillet and fry for 3 to 4 minutes. Turn the seitan over and fry for another 3 to 4 minutes, or until golden brown on both sides. Remove from the oil with a slotted spoon to a paper towel–covered plate to drain.

To prepare the Cream Gravy: Pour all of the oil from the pan except 3 tablespoons and the pan drippings. Heat in the skillet over medium heat. Add the flour and Southern Seasoning and cook for 3 to 5 minutes, stirring and scraping the bottom of the pan with a wooden spoon to loosen any browned bits from the seitan and lightly browning the flour. Stir in the water, soy milk, and Vegetarian Worcestershire Sauce. Increase the heat to high and bring the mixture to a boil to thicken it. Boil for 5 minutes, stirring, until the gravy is thick and smooth. Serve with the chicken-fried seitan.

SMOTHERED CHICKEN SEITAN WITH VEGGIE GRAVY

MAKES 8 SERVINGS

This old Southern recipe has been given a modern twist with the addition of chicken-flavored seitan. If you can't find chicken-flavored seitan, you can use plain seitan with good results because of the flavor added by the poultry seasoning in this recipe.

VEGGIE GRAVY

1	tablespoon olive oil
1	tablespoon butter
1	yellow onion, peeled and finely chopped
3	cloves garlic, peeled and minced
2	ribs celery, finely chopped
1	teaspoon salt
1	teaspoon onion powder
½	teaspoon dried tarragon
½	teaspoon dried thyme
2	cups vegetable broth
3	tablespoons cornstarch
2	cups frozen mixed vegetables

CHICKEN SEITAN

2	cups uncooked long-grain white rice
½	cup whole wheat or all-purpose flour
2	teaspoons poultry seasoning
1	teaspoon salt
1	teaspoon freshly ground black pepper
⅛	teaspoon cayenne pepper
2	pounds chicken-flavored seitan, drained, patted dry, and cut into ½-inch-thick pieces
¼	cup vegetable oil
2	tablespoons butter

To prepare the Veggie Gravy: Heat the oil and butter in a large saucepan over medium heat. Add the onion and cook for 10 minutes, stirring occasionally. Add the garlic, celery, salt, onion powder, tarragon, and thyme and cook for 5 minutes. Stir in 1 cup of the vegetable broth and cook for 5 minutes.

Combine the remaining 1 cup vegetable broth and the cornstarch in a small bowl until well-blended. Increase the heat to high and bring the onion mixture to a boil. Stir in the broth mixture and cook, stirring, until the sauce starts to thicken. Reduce the heat to low and add the mixed vegetables. Cook for 10 minutes, stirring occasionally.

To prepare the Chicken Seitan: Prepare the rice according to package directions.

Meanwhile, combine the flour, poultry seasoning, salt, black pepper, and cayenne pepper in a zip-top plastic bag. Seal the bag and shake well. Add the seitan to the bag, seal, and shake well to coat the pieces.

Heat the oil and butter in a large skillet over medium heat until hot but not smoking. Shake off the excess flour from the seitan and place in the oil. Fry for 3 to 4 minutes per side, or until golden brown. Serve over the rice and covered with the veggie gravy.

SWEET POTATOES WITH PEANUTS À LA CARVER

MAKES 8 SERVINGS

This recipe calls for two of George Washington Carver's contributions to the salvation of Southern agriculture: sweet potatoes and peanuts.

4	medium sweet potatoes
⅔	cups plain soy milk
¼	cup smooth peanut butter
2	tablespoons light brown sugar
¼	teaspoon ground cinnamon
¼	teaspoon salt
½	teaspoon freshly grated nutmeg
½	cup roasted peanuts

Preheat the oven to 425 degrees.

Place the sweet potatoes on a baking sheet or in a baking pan. Bake for 50 to 60 minutes, or until fork-tender. Or, place the sweet potatoes in a spoke arrangement with the smallest ends toward the middle on a microwaveable plate. Microwave for 20 to 30 minutes, or until fork-tender.

When the sweet potatoes are cool enough to handle, slice each one in half lengthwise. Scoop out the flesh and place it in a large bowl, leaving the shells intact. Mash the flesh. Add the soy milk, peanut butter, brown sugar, cinnamon, and salt and beat with an electric mixer on medium speed until fluffy. Spoon the mixture into the shells. Sprinkle with the nutmeg and peanuts and place on the prepared baking sheet.

Bake for 10 minutes, or until lightly browned. Or, place the filled shells on a microwaveable plate and microwave for 4 minutes.

SOUTHERN-STYLE MUSTARD GREENS AND BLACK-EYED PEAS

MAKES 6 SERVINGS

You can't eat this dish without softly slurring your words and slowing down your pace. The combination is pure Southern and rooted in African traditions. This is a perfect dish to serve with Hoe Cakes (page 187).

2	quarts water
2	tablespoons olive oil
3	teaspoons salt
1	bunch (1½ pounds and 6 to 10 inches long) mustard greens, chopped into bite-sized pieces
3	large cloves garlic, peeled and minced
1	yellow onion, peeled and chopped
1	rib celery with leaves, thinly sliced
1	small red bell pepper, seeded, ribs removed, and chopped
1	can (28 ounces) diced tomatoes, drained and juice reserved
4	sprigs fresh thyme, stems trimmed and discarded
2	bay leaves
1½	teaspoons sugar
½	teaspoon freshly ground black pepper
¼	teaspoon crushed red-pepper flakes
2	cans (15 ounces each) black-eyed peas, rinsed and drained

Bring the water, 1 tablespoon of the oil, and 1 teaspoon of the salt to boil in a large pot over medium-high heat. Add the greens. Reduce the heat to low, cover, and cook for 5 to 8 minutes, or until the greens are bright green and wilted. Drain the greens in a colander and set aside.

Heat the remaining 1 tablespoon oil in a large skillet over medium-high heat. Add the garlic, onion, celery, and bell pepper. Sauté for 10 minutes, stirring often, or until the vegetables are soft and beginning to brown.

Add the tomatoes, thyme, bay leaves, sugar, black pepper, red-pepper flakes, and the remaining 2 teaspoons salt to the pot. Partially cover the pot with a lid. Reduce the heat to low and simmer gently for 5 minutes, adding the reserved tomato juice, ¼ cup at a time, if the mixture appears dry. Add the peas and greens and stir well. Partially cover and cook for 15 minutes, stirring often. Taste the greens and beans for seasoning and tenderness, adding more seasoning or cooking longer, if necessary. Remove and discard the bay leaves before serving.

STEWED TOMATOES WITH DUMPLINGS

MAKES 6 SERVINGS

Dumplings have always been a part of African-American cooking. African versions were made out of cornmeal, but the results were the same: a savory dough that perfectly complements the juices that it's stewed in. I've found that this unusual combination of tomatoes and dumplings is a great way to use the abundant tomatoes I grow in my garden.

1¼	cups + 2 tablespoons butter or margarine
2	ribs celery, chopped
1	large yellow onion, peeled and chopped
1	large green bell pepper, seeded, ribs removed, and chopped
2	bay leaves
8	medium or large beefsteak tomatoes, peeled and quartered
2	teaspoons brown sugar
1½	teaspoons salt
1¼	teaspoons freshly ground black pepper
1¼	teaspoons freshly grated nutmeg
4	leaves fresh basil, torn
1	cup whole wheat or all-purpose flour
1½	teaspoons baking powder
1½	teaspoons salt
1	large egg, lightly beaten
1⅓	cups plain soy milk
4	sprigs parsley, minced

Melt 1¼ cups of the butter or margarine in a large pot over medium-high heat. Add the celery, onion, bell pepper, and bay leaves. Sauté for 10 minutes, or until the onion and bell pepper are tender. Stir in the tomatoes, brown sugar, salt, black pepper, and nutmeg. Bring to a boil. Reduce the heat to low and simmer. Stir in the basil.

Combine the flour, baking powder, and salt in a medium bowl. Cut in the remaining 2 tablespoons butter or margarine with a pastry blender or fork until the mixture is crumbly. Add the egg, milk, and parsley. Stir until the flour mixture is moistened and forms a soft dough. Drop the dough by tablespoonfuls into the simmering tomato mixture. Increase the heat to medium, cover, and cook the tomatoes and dumplings for 20 minutes. Remove and discard the bay leaves before serving.

Cooking Tip: To peel the tomatoes, immerse them in boiling water for 30 seconds, then into cold water for 30 seconds. The skin should slip off easily.

VEGETABLE MEDLEY AND CORNMEAL PANCAKES

The spicy vegetable topping really makes these old-fashioned pancakes sing. The pancakes are also wonderful for breakfast with syrup.

VEGETABLE MEDLEY

2	tablespoons olive oil
2	tablespoons butter
1	large onion, peeled and chopped
1	large green bell pepper, seeded, ribs removed, and chopped
1	jalapeño chile pepper, seeded, ribs removed, and chopped (wear plastic gloves when handling)
1	package (8 ounces) frozen and thawed corn kernels
1	package (16 ounces) frozen and thawed chopped okra, or 1 quart fresh okra, tips and stems removed and sliced
4	medium tomatoes, chopped
½	cup vegetable broth
1	teaspoon salt
1	teaspoon freshly ground black pepper
½	teaspoon sugar
⅛	teaspoon cayenne pepper
4	leaves fresh basil, torn

CORNMEAL PANCAKES

¾	cup cornmeal
½	cup whole wheat or all-purpose flour
1	teaspoon sugar
1	teaspoon baking powder
¾	teaspoon salt
¼	teaspoon freshly grated nutmeg
1	large egg, beaten
1	cup vanilla-flavored soy milk
3	tablespoons butter, melted
1	tablespoon vegetable oil

To prepare the Vegetable Medley: Heat the oil and butter in a large saucepan over medium-high heat. Add the onion, bell pepper, and chile pepper. Sauté for 10 minutes, or until the onion is golden and the vegetables are tender. Stir in the corn, okra, tomatoes, vegetable broth, salt, black pepper, sugar, and cayenne pepper and bring the ingredients to a boil. Add the basil. Reduce the heat to low, cover, and cook for 20 minutes, stirring occasionally.

To prepare the Cornmeal Pancakes: Meanwhile, sift the cornmeal, flour, sugar, baking powder, salt, and nutmeg into a large bowl. Whisk the egg, soy milk, and butter into the cornmeal mixture. Stir until the ingredients are well-blended.

Heat the oil in a large skillet over medium heat. Working in batches, place 2 large tablespoons of the batter in the skillet to make 1 pancake. Cook for 2 minutes, or until bubbles appear around the edges and the bottom is lightly browned. Turn the pancake over and brown the other side lightly. Repeat to use the remaining batter. Place the pancakes on individual plates. Serve topped with the vegetable medley.

VEGGIE SCRAPPLE

MAKES 4 SERVINGS

This recipe is similar to many African dishes and a traditional Southern dish called scrapple. Scrapple contains small pieces of meat, the meat juices, cornmeal, and other seasoning. The mixture is pressed into a loaf pan, chilled, and then sliced and pan-fried. This vegetarian version makes a tasty main dish for a Sunday dinner.

3	tablespoons butter
1	tablespoon olive oil
1	small yellow onion, peeled and finely chopped
2	ribs celery, finely chopped
2	cloves garlic, peeled and minced
1	green or red bell pepper, seeded, ribs removed, and chopped
1	can (15 ounces) black-eyed peas, rinsed and drained
1	teaspoon salt
1	teaspoon freshly ground black pepper
1	teaspoon onion powder
⅛	teaspoon cayenne pepper
½	cup cornmeal
⅓	cup old-fashioned rolled oats (not quick-cooking)
2	cups vegetable broth

Butter an $8\frac{1}{2} \times 4\frac{1}{2}$-inch or $9 \times 5 \times 3$-inch loaf pan.

Heat 1 tablespoon of the butter and the oil in a large skillet over medium-high heat. Add the onion and sauté for 10 minutes. Add the celery, garlic, and bell pepper. Sauté for 7 minutes, or until the vegetables are tender.

Stir in the black-eyed peas, salt, black pepper, onion powder, and cayenne pepper. Cook for an additional 5 minutes. Add the cornmeal, oats, and vegetable broth. Stir until well-combined. Place the mixture in the prepared pan.

Bake for 45 minutes. Remove the pan to a rack and allow it to cool to room temperature. Cover and chill the scrapple for 4 hours or overnight.

Cut the scrapple into 1-inch-thick slices. Heat the remaining 2 tablespoons butter in a large skillet over medium-high heat. Working in batches, add the scrapple and fry for 3 to 4 minutes, or until lightly browned on both sides.

Cooking Tip: The scrapple is also delicious served cold, so if you prefer, you can skip the pan-frying step.

BAKED TOMATOES AND ONIONS
WITH CORNBREAD STUFFING

MAKES 12 SERVINGS

Cornbread stuffing, or dressing, is an old Southern tradition and a delicious way to use leftover cornbread and day-old sandwich bread. This recipe is also a wonderful holiday dish.

6	medium tomatoes
3	large Spanish onions, peeled
1½	cups crumbled cornbread
1½	cups crumbled dry day-old whole wheat bread
1½	cups vegetable broth
¼	cup melted butter
1	egg, beaten
2	ribs celery, finely chopped
1	green bell pepper, seeded, ribs removed, and finely chopped
2	teaspoons poultry seasoning
1	teaspoon freshly ground black pepper
1	teaspoon salt
¼	cup dried bread crumbs
¼	cup (1 ounce) freshly grated Parmesan cheese

Preheat the oven to 350 degrees.

Cut a thin slice off the top of each tomato. Scoop out the pulp from the tomatoes and discard the seeds. Set aside the tomato shells. Chop the pulp and place it in a large bowl.

Cut the onions in half horizontally. Remove the centers and set aside the onion shells. Chop the onion centers and place them in the bowl with the tomato pulp.

Add the cornbread, whole wheat bread, vegetable broth, butter, egg, celery, bell pepper, poultry seasoning, black pepper, and salt to the tomato pulp mixture. Stir until the ingredients are moist and well-blended.

Place the tomato and onion shells in a shallow baking dish. Fill the shells with the cornbread mixture. Sprinkle with the bread crumbs and cheese.

Bake for 20 minutes, or until the tomatoes and onions are tender.

HOE CAKES

For slaves working the fields—and usually not allowed to go back to their cabins to pre-pare something to eat—hoe cakes were an ingenious way of making a quick hot noon-time meal. The following narrative from an unknown slave advised this method: "Stand in the shade near the edge of the field. Light a fire from whatever brush and twigs there may be. On the greased side of the blade of your hoe, mix meal and water until it is thick enough to fry. Add salt if you remembered to bring any. Lean the hoe into the fire until the top side of the bread bubbles. Flip it and brown the other side. If you do it without a hoe, you have to make suitable changes in the kitchen." A cast-iron skillet is the suitable change I recommend, along with the addition of some short-ening and butter.

1   cup fine white cornmeal
1   tablespoon shortening
1   teaspoon salt
⅔   cup boiling water
4   tablespoons butter

Combine the cornmeal, shortening, and salt in a large bowl. Some lumps will remain. Slowly add the water in a slow, steady stream, stirring constantly. Mix well. The mixture should be soft and smooth, but not wet.

Melt the butter in a large heavy skillet over high heat. Reduce the heat to low. Scoop up 2 tablespoons of the dough and pat it into a flat, round cake about 4 inches in diameter. The imprint of your fingers should remain in the hoe cakes when formed. Increase the heat to medium. Working in batches, fry the hoe cakes in the oil for 2 to 3 minutes per side, or until golden brown.

Cover pancakes with a dish towel to keep them warm.

ANGEL BISCUITS WITH FRIED APPLES

MAKES 12 SERVINGS

These delicate biscuits are similar in taste to an old recipe that is popular in the South. They're tender and nutritious. Work with the dough as gently as possible for fluffy biscuits. Serve the apples like you would a thick jam or jelly to spread on or eat with the biscuits.

ANGEL BISCUITS

1	cup soft wheat or white self-rising flour
3	tablespoons cream cheese or soy cream cheese, softened
2	tablespoons butter
⅓	cup plain soy milk

FRIED APPLES

1	stick (½ cup) butter or ½ cup soy margarine
6	Rome apples, peeled, cored, and cut into ½ inch slices, or 2 cans (20 ounces) sliced apples
½	cup sugar
½	teaspoon freshly squeezed lemon juice
⅛	teaspoon ground cinnamon
⅛	teaspoon freshly grated nutmeg
¼	cup water
1	teaspoon lemon zest

To prepare the Angel Biscuits: Preheat the oven to 425 degrees. Coat a baking sheet with cooking spray.

Place the flour, cream cheese, and butter in a medium bowl. Using a fork, blend the ingredients together until the mixture is crumbly. Gradually stir in the milk, 2 tablespoons at a time, until a soft dough forms. Turn the dough out onto a lightly floured board.

Gently knead the dough 4 or 5 times. Lightly pat out the dough to a $\frac{1}{2}$-inch thickness. Using a round 2-inch cutter, cut out biscuit rounds. Reroll the remaining pieces of dough and cut into additional biscuits. Place the biscuits 2 inches apart on the prepared baking sheet.

Bake for 8 minutes, or until lightly browned on the bottom. Serve warm with the fried apples.

To prepare the Fried Apples: Melt the butter in a large skillet over high heat. Add the apples and cook for 8 to 10 minutes, or until still slightly crisp but becoming tender. Stir in the sugar, lemon juice, cinnamon, and nutmeg and cook for 2 minutes, stirring occasionally. Add water and lemon zest. Reduce the heat to low, cover, and cook for 8 minutes, or until the apples are tender. Serve 1 to 2 heaping tablespoons of the fried apples with each biscuit.

CORNBREAD

As one of the many nourishing dishes slave cooks learned how to make out of their rations of coarse cornmeal, cornbread has a special place on the African-American table. This is one of my favorite recipes. And when mixed with seasoned bread crumbs, it is the secret to fabulous dressing. The golden-crisp crust you'll get on this cornbread is reason enough to invest in a cast-iron skillet if you don't already own one.

⅓ cup shortening
½ cup cornmeal
½ cup whole wheat or all-purpose flour
3 teaspoons baking powder
1 egg, beaten
⅓ cup water
⅓ cup sugar
½ teaspoon salt
⅔ cup evaporated milk

Preheat the oven to 400 degrees.

Place the shortening in a cast-iron skillet or heavy 8 × 8-inch baking pan. Melt the shortening in the skillet or pan. Set aside.

Combine the cornmeal, flour, baking powder, egg, water, sugar, salt, and milk in a large bowl. Mix well. Pour half of the melted shortening into the batter. Mix well. Pour the batter into the skillet. The hot shortening in the pan will make the edges of the cornbread crispy.

Bake for 15 to 20 minutes, or until the top is brown, the sides are crisp, and the tip of a knife inserted in the center comes out clean.

SPOON BREAD

A Southern dish with African roots, spoon bread is similar to the pone type of breads commonly found in African and Caribbean cooking. It got its name because it is so soft and pudding-like that it must be served and eaten with a spoon.

2½	cups plain soy milk
2	tablespoons butter
1	teaspoon salt
1	cup cornmeal
3	large egg yolks, whites reserved
½	cup heavy cream
⅛	teaspoon cream of tartar

Grease an 8 × 8-inch baking dish with cooking spray.

Combine the soy milk, butter, and salt in a heavy saucepan over medium heat. Reduce the heat to low and slowly whisk in the cornmeal, whisking constantly to prevent lumps. Increase the heat to medium and cook for 3 to 4 minutes, whisking constantly, until the mixture is thick and smooth. Remove the pan from the heat. Set aside to cool.

Whisk the egg yolks and cream together in a small bowl. Slowly whisk the egg mixture into the cornmeal mixture.

Place the egg whites and cream of tartar in a small, clean glass bowl. (Do not use the bowl that the egg yolks were in, because the egg whites will not peak.) With an electric mixer on high speed, beat until stiff peaks form. Gradually fold the egg whites into the cornmeal mixture. Scrape the spoon bread mixture into the prepared baking dish.

Bake for 25 to 35 minutes, or until the bread rises, turns golden brown on top, and a knife tip inserted in the middle comes out clean.

ETHNIC-STYLE GINGERBREAD

MAKES 16 SERVINGS

Gingerbread is an old Southern recipe. I like to serve this moist and delicious version topped with a spoonful of applesauce and whipped cream.

8	ounces soft, silken tofu, drained
½	cup molasses
¼	cup sugar
¼	cup butter, softened
1	cup all-purpose flour
½	cup whole wheat flour
1	teaspoon baking powder
½	teaspoon baking soda
¼	teaspoon salt
2	teaspoons ground ginger
1	teaspoon ground cinnamon
½	teaspoon ground cloves

Preheat the oven to 350 degrees. Lightly grease an 8-inch baking pan with cooking spray.

Combine the tofu, molasses, sugar, and butter in a medium bowl until well-blended.

Sift the flour, whole wheat flour, baking powder, baking soda, and salt into a medium bowl. Add the tofu mixture, ginger, cinnamon, and cloves. Pour the mixture into the prepared baking pan.

Bake for 35 minutes, or until the top springs back when lightly pressed. Remove to a rack and cool in the pan for 10 minutes. Cut the gingerbread into 16 squares. Gently remove the squares from the pan and store in an airtight container.

CREAMY RICE PUDDING

MAKES 8 SERVINGS

Rice puddings are a traditional dessert on African-American tables. Adding soy milk and yogurt increases the flavor and the health benefits.

- 2 cups vanilla-flavored soy milk
- 1 cup short-grain white rice
- 2 cups plain soy milk
- 1 cup vanilla soy yogurt
- ½ cup sugar
- ½ cup raisins
- 2 teaspoons ground cinnamon

Combine the soy milk and rice in a large saucepan over high heat. Bring the mixture to a boil. Reduce the heat to low and simmer for 10 minutes. Add the plain soy milk, yogurt, sugar, and raisins. Increase the heat to high and bring the mixture back to a boil, stirring constantly. Reduce the heat to low and simmer for 15 minutes, stirring occasionally, to keep the mixture smooth and well-blended.

Place the pudding in individual dessert dishes and cool to room temperature. Cover with plastic wrap and refrigerate. Serve sprinkled with the cinnamon.

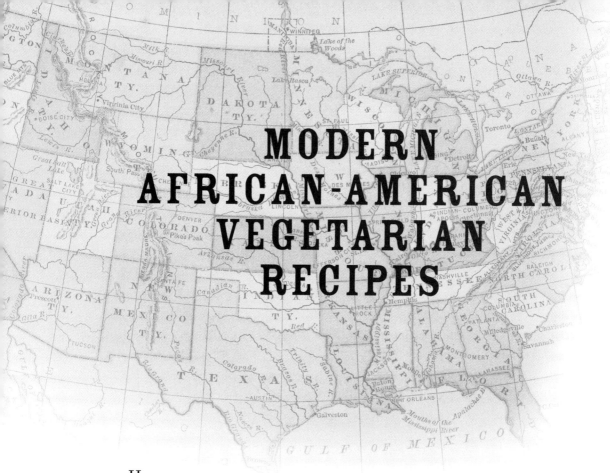

MODERN AFRICAN-AMERICAN VEGETARIAN RECIPES

HAVING WOUND OUR WAY ACROSS CONTINENTS and centuries, here we are at the present, where I'm pleased to offer my favorite modern African-American vegetarian recipes.

All of the recipes in this chapter have special memories attached to them. I prepared Heritage Dip in small bookstores using an electric skillet during my first cookbook tour in 1994 and many times since on national television shows. I'll never forget the sheer delight of the initially skeptical radio host who sampled my Texas Caviar during an interview in Washington,

D.C. I had to try to answer questions without laughing at his enthusiastic reaction!

The recipe for Southwestern Tortilla Soup is based on one of my favorite family dinners growing up; it is still one of my favorite ethnic vegetarian entrées. The Jalapeño Cornbread comes from my Aunt Florine, who prepared it for a family reunion and was happy to share the recipe with anyone who wanted it. You can taste her generous spirit in every bite.

A good meal has a wonderful way of crossing cultures, borders, racial divides, and family discord to fuse people together in harmony around a dinner table. One of the challenges we face in changing from a meat-centered diet to a vegetable-based one is the sensory and emotional connections we have with the foods we eat. Smells and tastes trigger memories. The decision to embrace a vegetarian diet is as much a decision to make new food memories as it is to try new ingredients and recipes.

While holidays, family gatherings, special occasions, and your evening meals may be different now that you've moved toward a vegetarian lifestyle, one thing remains unchanged: it's not just a meal you're creating, it's a priceless memory. Whether you are eating alone or with a crowd, make an effort to make each meal a celebration of life. It's the way of our ancestors and tradition that should continue from generation to generation.

HERITAGE DIP

Black-eyed peas and greens, two of the foods that were introduced to America by Africans, are included in this appetizing dip. The addition of soft tofu makes it even more nutritious and delicious.

- 1 package (10 ounces) frozen turnip greens
- 1 can (15 ounces) black-eyed peas, rinsed and drained
- 2 teaspoons salt
- 2 teaspoons freshly ground black pepper
- Zest of 1 lemon
- 2 tablespoons olive oil
- 2 tablespoons butter
- 2 ribs celery, chopped
- 1 small purple onion, peeled and chopped
- 1 tablespoon Caribbean hot sauce, such as Pickapeppa Sauce
- 1 teaspoon garlic powder
- 1 teaspoon onion powder
- 1 can (10 ounces) cream of mushroom soup
- 4 ounces cream cheese
- 4 ounces soft, silken tofu, drained
- Sesame seed wafers

Prepare the turnip greens according to the package directions. Drain and place in a food processor or blender along with the black-eyed peas, 1 teaspoon of the salt, 1 teaspoon of the pepper, and the lemon zest. Process to puree the greens and black-eyed peas until fairly smooth but leaving some texture.

Heat the oil and butter in a large skillet over medium-high heat. Add the celery and onion and sauté for 10 minutes, or until the vegetables are soft. Reduce the heat to low. Add the greens mixture, hot sauce, garlic powder, onion powder, the remaining 1 teaspoon salt, and the remaining 1 teaspoon pepper. Cook for 5 minutes. Add the soup, cream cheese, and tofu, stirring to blend the ingredients. Cook for 10 minutes, stirring occasionally, or until the ingredients are smooth and well-blended. Serve the dip with the sesame seed wafers.

CORN CAKES WITH TEXAS CAVIAR

These delicate corn cakes and the delightful black-eyed pea relish we call Texas Caviar make a fabulous appetizer. The "caviar" must be prepared at least 2 days in advance, but it keeps for several weeks. You can make the cakes as instructed and then place 2 tablespoons of the caviar on top, or make the cakes larger and serve this dish as a first course.

TEXAS CAVIAR

- 1 cup vegetable oil
- ¼ cup red wine vinegar
- 2 cans (16 ounces each) black-eyed peas, rinsed and drained
- 1 small purple onion, peeled and chopped
- 1 small green bell pepper, seeded, ribs removed, and chopped
- 1 clove garlic, peeled and crushed
- 1 teaspoon salt
- 1 teaspoon freshly ground black pepper
- 1 teaspoon onion powder
- ⅛ teaspoon cayenne pepper

CORN CAKES

- ½ cup whole wheat or all-purpose flour
- ½ cup cornmeal
- 1 tablespoon sugar
- 1 teaspoon baking powder
- 1 teaspoon salt
- ⅛ teaspoon cayenne pepper
- 1 cup cream-style corn
- 2 green onions, trimmed and finely chopped
- 1 egg, beaten
- ¼ cup vegetable oil
- ½ cup plain soy milk

To prepare the Texas Caviar: Place all ingredients in a container with tight-fitting lid. Seal and shake well. Refrigerate for 2 days. Remove and discard the garlic clove. Shake the container once per day to blend the ingredients.

To prepare the Corn Cakes: Sift the flour, cornmeal, sugar, baking powder, salt, and cayenne pepper into a medium bowl. Combine the corn, green onions, egg, and 2 tablespoons of the oil together until well-blended. Add the corn mixture to the flour mixture, stirring until well-blended. Stir in the soy milk. The mixture should be the consistency of a thick pancake batter. Add a little more milk, if needed, to thin the mixture.

Heat the remaining 2 tablespoons oil in a heavy skillet. Working in batches, place about 3 heaping tablespoons of the batter into the skillet to make 1 cake. Cook for 3 to 5 minutes, or until 1 or 2 bubbles appear on top and the bottom is golden brown. Turn the cake over and brown the other side lightly. Repeat to use the remaining batter.

Cooking Tip: The Texas Caviar will keep in the refrigerator for 2 weeks. It also works well as a dip for tortilla chips or pita bread.

GREEN BEAN AND SESAME SALAD

MAKES 8 SERVINGS

The Wolof name for sesame is benne. *Sesame seeds occupy an important place in African-American culinary history—the many uses for sesame seeds and sesame oil were introduced to America by African slaves.*

2 teaspoons salt
2 pounds young green beans, stemmed
¼ cup olive oil
¼ cup sesame seeds, toasted
2 tablespoons freshly squeezed lemon juice
2 cloves garlic, peeled and minced
1 teaspoon freshly ground black pepper
½ teaspoon red-pepper flakes

Bring a large pot of water and 1 teaspoon of the salt to a rapid boil over high heat. Place the beans in the water and cook for 3 to 5 minutes, or until the beans are tender. Do not overcook. Drain the beans in a large colander. Plunge the beans into a bowl of ice water for 2 to 3 minutes to stop the cooking and retain the color. Drain thoroughly.

Combine the oil, sesame seeds, lemon juice, garlic, black pepper, red-pepper flakes, and the remaining 1 teaspoon salt in a large bowl. Add the green beans and toss gently to combine. Serve at room temperature.

SWEET SALAD

This tasty combination of sweet potatoes, sweet peas, and sweet corn is a nice change from standard potato salad.

2	teaspoons salt
2	large sweet potatoes, scrubbed and quartered
1	cup fresh or frozen and thawed peas
1	cup fresh or frozen and thawed corn kernels
½	cup Garlic-Tofu Mayonnaise (page 254), dairy mayonnaise, or salad dressing
½	cup sweet pickle relish
4	sprigs parsley, chopped
1	tablespoon Dijon mustard
1	teaspoon freshly ground black pepper
4	eggs, hard-cooked and chopped
2	ribs celery, finely chopped
1	small purple onion, peeled and finely chopped
1	cup (4 ounces) shredded Cheddar cheese

Bring a large saucepan of cold water and 1 teaspoon of the salt to a boil over high heat. Add the sweet potatoes and boil for 15 minutes. Add the peas and corn. Cook for an additional 5 minutes, or until the sweet potatoes are tender. Drain the vegetables in a large colander and cool under cold running water. Shake off any excess water and set the vegetables aside to drain. Peel the skin off the potatoes, chop the flesh, and set aside.

Combine the mayonnaise, relish, parsley, mustard, pepper, and the remaining 1 teaspoon salt in a large bowl. Add the eggs, celery, onion, and cheese and mix thoroughly to blend. Add the sweet potato mixture to the bowl. Stir the ingredients gently so that the potatoes don't break apart. Add more mayonnaise, salt, and pepper, if needed, to moisten and season the salad.

SOUL SUSHI

Contrary to what many people think, sushi *doesn't mean raw fish;* sashimi *means raw fish. Sushi is defined as a marriage of rice and vinegar with other ingredients. Soul Sushi is composed of sesame oil, sesame seeds, and sweet potatoes, three delicious culinary contributions from Africa to America. When mixed with a few other ingredients and encased in a California roll, which has the rice on the outside, Soul Sushi makes a fabulous ethnic vegetarian appetizer or evening meal—so don't let the detailed instructions discourage you from preparing it.*

1	cup uncooked short-grain white rice
1	cup + 2 tablespoons rice wine vinegar
2	tablespoons toasted sesame oil
3	ribs celery, cut into halves, then into 16 thin lengthwise strips
2	green onions, trimmed and cut into strips
1	small cucumber, such as English, hothouse, or Haas, halved lengthwise, seeded, and cut into 16 thin lengthwise strips
1	teaspoon sugar
1	teaspoon salt
1	can (15 ounces) sweet potatoes, drained
¼	cup chopped fresh cilantro
1	teaspoon soy sauce
4	sheets nori sea vegetable wrappers
2	tablespoons sesame seeds, toasted
	Pickled ginger, sliced (optional)
	Wasabi sauce (optional)
	Soy sauce (optional)

Prepare the rice according to package directions. Cool completely.

Combine 1 cup of the vinegar and the oil to make a marinade in a medium bowl. Add the celery, green onions, and cucumber, turning to coat with the marinade. Marinate at room temperature for 3 to 4 hours. Remove the vegetables to a colander to drain. Set aside.

Combine the sugar, salt, and the remaining 2 tablespoons vinegar in a small bowl. Slowly pour the vinegar mixture over the rice, about 2 tablespoons at a time. Using a large wooden spoon, mix the rice with a slicing motion to mix in the vinegar. The rice should be moist but not wet; add another 1 to 2 tablespoons vinegar if needed. Cover the bowl with a clean, damp cloth to keep the rice moist. Set aside.

Place the sweet potatoes, cilantro, and soy sauce in a food processor or blender. Process to mix until smooth and creamy.

Fold 4 sheets of nori evenly in half and cut them to make 8 sheets.

Place a piece of plastic wrap, 2 to 3 inches larger than the half sheets of nori, on a flat surface. Fill a small bowl with water to dip your hands in to keep them damp so the ingredients won't stick to them.

Place ½ cup of the rice on top of the plastic wrap, pressing out the rice to the size of a sheet of nori. Place a sheet of nori on top of the rice.

Spread ¼ cup of the sweet potato mixture on top of the nori. Sprinkle the sesame seeds on top of the sweet potatoes. Evenly divide the celery, green onions, and cucumber among the nori, on the part of the sushi that's closest to you. If some of the vegetable strips extend over one end of the nori, that's fine. It adds interest to the finished dish when the sushi is cut and arranged.

Use your fingers to hold the vegetables in place and begin rolling the sushi, using the plastic wrap to help with the process. Stop after each turn and squeeze along the entire roll to make sure that it's even and tight. Continue rolling, stopping to squeeze the sushi roll, until you get to the end of the nori sheet. The roll should be tight with the ingredients in the center. Moisten the nori sheet with a little water and press the edges together to seal. Place the roll, seam side down, on a plate. Repeat to roll the remaining sushi. Place the sushi rolls in the refrigerator to chill for 30 minutes before cutting.

Wet a knife and cut the sushi into 1½-inch-thick slices, with the vegetable pieces extending out of one end. Arrange the sushi rolls upright on a platter. Serve cold with the ginger, wasabi sauce, and soy sauce as condiments, if desired.

SOUTHWESTERN TORTILLA SOUP

MAKES 8 SERVINGS

I've spent most of my life in the Southwest. I grew up with this wonderful soup and the handmade flat bread that it is named for. The crispy tortilla strips are a great topping, and the avocado slices and cheese are delicious condiments.

½	cup vegetable oil
1	medium yellow onion, peeled and chopped
1	large green bell pepper, seeded, ribs removed, and chopped
2	medium tomatoes, chopped
1	yellow squash, chopped
1½	teaspoon salt
1	teaspoon freshly ground black pepper
1	teaspoon chili powder
6	cups vegetable broth
2	ears corn, shucked and cut into quarters or 2 cups frozen corn kernels
8	corn or flour tortillas, cut into ¼-inch strips
2	large ripe, firm avocados, peeled, seeded, and sliced
1	cup (4 ounces) shredded Cheddar or Monterey Jack cheese

Heat ¼ cup of the oil in a large stock pot over medium-high heat. Add the onion and the bell pepper and sauté for 10 minutes, or until tender. Stir in the tomatoes, squash, 1 teaspoon of the salt, the black pepper, and chili powder. Add the vegetable broth and corn.

Increase the heat to high and bring the mixture to a boil. Reduce the heat to low, cover, and simmer for 30 minutes, stirring occasionally.

Heat the remaining ¼ cup oil in a large skillet over high heat until hot but not smoking. Working in batches, add the tortilla strips and fry for 10 to 15 seconds, or until crisp and golden. Remove from the oil to a paper towel–covered plate to drain. Sprinkle the tortilla strips with the remaining ½ teaspoon salt.

Serve the soup in individual bowls topped with the avocado, cheese, and tortilla strips.

BLACK BEAN CHILI

MAKES 6 SERVINGS

I love a hearty bowl of chili in the wintertime, but this recipe is good any time of year. Use this chili as a topper for a baked potato, as a filling for a flour tortilla, or alone with a salad and cornbread. Don't hesitate to make this recipe ahead of time and let it sit in the refrigerator for a few days—the more time flavors have to blend, the better it tastes.

2	tablespoons olive oil
2	tablespoons butter
1	large yellow onion, peeled and chopped
1	large green bell pepper, seeded, ribs removed, and chopped
1	jalapeño chile pepper, seeded and minced (wear plastic gloves when handling)
2	cloves garlic, peeled and minced
1	can (14 ounces) diced tomatoes and green chiles
1	tablespoon chili powder
1	teaspoon ground cumin
1	teaspoon dried oregano
⅛	teaspoon cayenne pepper
2	cans (15 ounces each) black beans, rinsed and drained
1	cup spicy tomato juice
3	tablespoons brown sugar
1	cup fresh or frozen and thawed corn kernels
¼	cup chopped fresh cilantro

Heat the oil and butter in a large pot over medium-high heat. Add the onion and sauté for 10 minutes to infuse the oil with flavor.

Add the bell pepper, chile pepper, and garlic and cook for 5 minutes, or until the vegetables are soft. Reduce the heat to low. Stir in the tomatoes (with juice), chili powder, cumin, oregano, and cayenne pepper and cook for 5 minutes. Stir in the beans, tomato juice, and brown sugar and simmer for 15 minutes. Add the corn and 2 tablespoons of the cilantro and cook for 5 minutes. Place the chili in individual serving bowls. Sprinkle with the remaining 2 tablespoons cilantro.

BEAN PATTIES

MAKES 8 PATTIES

You might want to double this recipe and freeze the patties between sheets of plastic wrap for quick meals. They're best when served as main dish with a crisp salad.

1   can (15 ounces) kidney beans, rinsed and drained
4   ounces firm, silken tofu, drained
1   egg, beaten
1   cup dried whole wheat bread crumbs
1   tablespoon ketchup
1   teaspoon Vegetarian Worcestershire Sauce (page 255) or prepared vegetarian Worcestershire sauce
1   teaspoon salt
1   teaspoon freshly ground black pepper
5   tablespoons vegetable oil
1   yellow onion, peeled and grated
2   cloves garlic, peeled and crushed
1   tablespoon brown sugar
½   teaspoon ground cumin
½   teaspoon dried oregano
   Flour for coating patties

Place the beans in a medium bowl and mash slightly. Add the tofu, egg, bread crumbs, ketchup, Worcestershire sauce, salt, and pepper. Mix well.

Heat 2 tablespoons of the oil in a large skillet over medium-high heat. Add the onion, garlic, brown sugar, cumin, and oregano. Sauté for 10 minutes, or until the onion is soft. Place the onion mixture in the bowl with the beans and stir to combine.

Lightly dust your hands with the flour to prevent the mixture from sticking. Form the mixture into 8 patties. Coat the patties lightly with flour. Place on a plate and chill for 20 to 30 minutes.

Heat the remaining 3 tablespoons oil in the same skillet over medium heat. Working in batches, add the patties and fry for 3 to 4 minutes, turning once, or until lightly browned on both sides.

VEGGIE BURGERS

Anysa, my sweet but picky granddaughter, has grown to love vegetarian dishes, especially if they resemble something that comes in a paper bag with a toy inside. Serve these on a sesame seed bun with your favorite condiments for that "drive-thru" experience.

1	can (15 ounces) chickpeas, rinsed and drained
1	small yellow onion, peeled and quartered
1⅓	cup old-fashioned rolled oats (not quick-cooking)
1	cup water
1	teaspoon salt
1	teaspoon freshly ground black pepper
1	teaspoon garlic powder
½	tablespoon soy sauce
½	tablespoon ketchup
	Flour for dusting burgers
2	tablespoons olive oil

Place the beans and onion in a food processor. Process to grind until the texture is coarse. Add the oats, water, salt, black pepper, garlic powder, soy sauce, and ketchup. Pulse for 10 seconds. Scrape down the sides of the bowl and mix the ingredients. Remove the bowl from the food processor and place it in the refrigerator to chill for 25 to 30 minutes.

Lightly flour your hands and form the mixture into 6 burgers. Heat the oil in a large skillet over medium heat. Working in batches if necessary, place the burgers into the pan, pressing them as they cook. Cook for 4 minutes per side, or until golden brown on both sides

COLLARD GREENS QUICHE

MAKES 8 SERVINGS

Quiche is a French creation, but this one has a Southern drawl. I often keep extra piecrust dough on hand so I can make this recipe quickly. Good-quality ready-made crust is also fine.

1	Easy Piecrust (page 218) or 1 (9-inch) prepared piecrust
1	package (10 ounces) frozen chopped collard greens
2	tablespoons olive oil
1	red or green bell pepper, seeded, ribs removed, and chopped
1	small purple onion, peeled and chopped
6	eggs
1	cup plain soy milk
1	teaspoon salt
1	teaspoon freshly ground black pepper
1	teaspoon dried tarragon
½	teaspoon dried oregano
⅛	teaspoon cayenne pepper
½	cup (2 ounces) shredded Swiss cheese
½	cup (2 ounces) shredded mild Cheddar cheese

Preheat the oven to 350 degrees. Prick the bottom and the sides of the piecrust with a fork. Partially bake the crust for 12 minutes, or until light brown. Remove to a rack and let cool.

Prepare the collard greens according to package directions. Drain in a large colander and squeeze dry. Set the greens aside.

Heat the oil in a small skillet over medium-high heat. Add the bell pepper and onion and sauté for 10 minutes, or until tender. Set the vegetables aside to cool.

Break the eggs into a large bowl. Add the onion mixture, soy milk, salt, black pepper, tarragon, oregano, and cayenne pepper and whisk the ingredients to combine. Add the greens, stirring until well-blended.

Sprinkle the bottom of the crust with the Swiss cheese. Pour the egg mixture into the crust. Sprinkle with the Cheddar cheese. Bake for 55 to 60 minutes, or until a knife inserted in the center comes out clean. Remove from the oven and let stand for 10 minutes before cutting.

GRILLED GREENS

MAKES 8 SERVINGS

Preparing food on the grill for a barbecue party (or 'cueing, as we say) is as much a part of summertime in Texas as the mosquitoes. 'Cueing vegetarian-style is easy and delicious. These uniquely prepared greens have a wonderful flavor. Wrapping them in foil harkens back to the African method of cooking food wrapped it banana leaves.

8	cups tightly packed trimmed spinach, kale, or collard greens
4	tablespoons water
3	tablespoons olive oil
2	tablespoons balsamic vinegar
4	cloves garlic, peeled and minced
1	red bell pepper, seeded, ribs removed, and thinly sliced
1	yellow onion, peeled and thinly sliced
1	teaspoon salt
1	teaspoon sugar
½	teaspoon cayenne pepper

Heat the grill according to the manufacturer's instructions.

In a medium bowl, combine the greens, water, oil, vinegar, garlic, bell pepper, onion, salt, sugar, and cayenne pepper. Place two 24-inch pieces of heavy-duty foil on top of each other and mound the seasoned greens in the center. Bring up two sides of the foil to meet in the center, pressing the edges together and then folding the foil over twice to make two (½-inch) folds. Allow room for the packet to fill with steam and expand. Fold the edges of each end together twice to make two (½-inch) folds. Press the edges together to seal.

Place the packet on the grill rack and grill for 10 to 12 minutes. Using oven mitts to protect your hands, remove the packet from the grill and open it carefully away from your face, allowing the hot steam to escape. The greens should be wilted and cooked through.

MIXED GREENS RISOTTO

MAKES 6 SERVINGS

Miss Betty, a well-known cook in Atlanta, Georgia, is the inspiration for this soulful risotto. I've taken quite a few liberties with her original recipe to make this a vegetarian dish, but the love she pours into it is still there.

2	medium yellow onions, peeled
4	cups vegetable broth
4	cloves
4	bay leaves
2	tablespoons olive oil
2	tablespoons butter
1	medium carrot, peeled and chopped
2	cloves garlic, peeled and minced
2	cups uncooked short-grain white rice (do not rinse)
3	sprigs fresh thyme, chopped and stems discarded, or 1 teaspoon dried
2	teaspoons salt
½	cup dry white wine
½	cup tomato sauce or marinara sauce
½	pound fresh spinach, chopped
½	pound fresh collard greens, chopped
½	cup (2 ounces) shredded sharp Cheddar cheese
1	teaspoon freshly ground black pepper
¾	cup (3 ounces) freshly grated Parmesan cheese
8	green onions, trimmed and chopped

Peel and quarter one of the onions. In a small pot, heat the vegetable broth over low heat. Add the onion quarters, cloves, and bay leaves and simmer gently. Set aside. Peel and chop the remaining onion and set it aside.

Heat the oil and butter in a large, wide nonreactive skillet over medium-low heat. Add the remaining onion, the carrot, and garlic and sauté for 5 minutes, or until the onion is softened. Add the rice, thyme, and 1 teaspoon of the salt. Stir well to coat the ingredients with the oil. Add the wine and simmer for 8 to 10 minutes, or until the liquid is absorbed, stirring constantly.

Add the tomato sauce and 1 cup of the broth mixture. Bring the mixture to a boil, then reduce the heat to low. Simmer for 2 to 3 minutes, stirring constantly, or until the liquid is absorbed by the rice. Add the spinach, collard greens, and 1 cup of the remaining broth mixture. Cook, stirring, for 2 to 3 minutes, or until the liquid is absorbed. Add the 1 cup of the remaining broth mixture, and cook for 2 to 3 minutes, stirring, or until the liquid is absorbed. Add the remaining broth to the rice mixture. Discard the onion, cloves, and bay leaves. Cook for 2 to 3 minutes, stirring, until the liquid is absorbed, the rice is creamy and soft, and the greens are tender.

Add the Cheddar cheese, the remaining 1 teaspoon salt, and the black pepper. Taste and add more seasoning if desired.

Place the risotto in individual dishes. Sprinkle with the Parmesan cheese and green onions.

PORTOBELLO MUSHROOMS
AND PARMESAN RICE TIMBALES

MAKES 8 SERVINGS

This is what I call "company food." It looks elegant, tastes delicious, and can be prepared quickly.

2	cups uncooked basmati rice
1	cup (4 ounces) freshly grated Parmesan cheese
	Zest of 1 small lemon
2½	teaspoons salt
1½	teaspoon freshly ground black pepper
4	portobello mushrooms (about 8 ounces each), stems removed, wiped clean
2	tablespoons olive oil
⅛	teaspoon cayenne pepper
4	large tomatoes, cut into ½-inch-thick slices
1	teaspoon sugar
1	can (15 ounces) black-eyed peas, rinsed and drained
1	tablespoon salsa
8	leaves fresh basil, torn

Prepare the rice according to package directions. Combine the rice, cheese, lemon zest, 1 teaspoon of the salt, and ½ teaspoon of the black pepper in a medium bowl.

Place a piece of waxed paper inside each of 8 ramekins or glass juice tumblers with the paper slightly overlapping the edges to ease removal of the timbales. Pack the rice mixture firmly into the ramekins, pressing in as much as you can. Set aside.

Slice the mushrooms at an angle into pieces that are ½-inch thick. Brush the slices with 1 tablespoon of the oil.

Heat the remaining 1 tablespoon oil in a heavy pan or cast-iron skillet or grill pan over high heat until hot but not smoking. Working in batches, add the mushroom slices and sear for 4 to 5 minutes. Turn the slices over and sear the other side for 3 to 4 minutes. Allow 1 minute between batches so that the skillet or pan can heat back up. Repeat to cook the remaining mushroom slices.

Remove the mushroom slices to a plate and sprinkle with the cayenne pepper, ½ teaspoon of the remaining salt, and ½ teaspoon of the remaining black pepper.

Working in batches, add the tomato slices to the skillet and sear for 2 to 3 minutes. Turn the slices over and sear the other side for 2 to 3 minutes. Remove the tomato slices to a plate. Sprinkle with ½ teaspoon of the sugar, ½ teaspoon of the remaining salt, and the remaining ½ teaspoon black pepper.

Heat the black-eyed peas in a pot over medium heat. Stir in the salsa, the remaining ½ teaspoon of salt, and the remaining ½ teaspoon sugar. Place the black-eyed peas in a food processor or blender. Leave the feed tube open on the food processor or the top slightly off the blender to allow air in and prevent overflow. Process to puree until smooth. Set aside.

Unmold the timbales onto the center of a serving plate. Remove the waxed paper and discard. Place alternating slices of the mushrooms and tomatoes around the rice timbales. Spoon the black-eyed pea puree around the edge of the vegetables. Sprinkle with the basil leaves.

BENNE CRACKERS

MAKES 1 DOZEN CRACKERS

Benne crackers are a West African recipe. Benne are sesame seeds. These little crackers are a delicious accompaniment to Texas Caviar (page 198) or Cucumber and Pepper Relish (page 5).

1	cup packed brown sugar
¼	cup butter, softened
1	egg, beaten
1	teaspoon freshly squeezed lemon juice
½	teaspoon vanilla extract
½	cup whole wheat or all-purpose flour
½	teaspoon baking powder
¼	teaspoon salt
1	cup sesame seeds, toasted

Preheat the oven to 325 degrees. Lightly oil a baking sheet.

Combine the brown sugar and butter in a food processor or large bowl. Process or beat with an electric mixer on medium speed until creamy. Add the egg, lemon juice, and vanilla extract and process or mix briefly to blend. Add the flour, baking powder, salt, and sesame seeds. Process or mix until well-combined. (The batter will be slightly lumpy.)

Drop the batter by rounded teaspoons onto the prepared baking sheet 2 inches apart. Bake for 15 minutes, or until the edges are browned.

AUNT FLORINE'S JALAPEÑO CORNBREAD

MAKES 8 SERVINGS

My glamorous Aunt Florine made this cornbread to rave reviews. I've adapted it ethnic-vegetarian—style with the addition of soy milk and soy sausage. I love serving it with chili or vegetable or lentil soups. My husband says he'd gladly make a meal of this delicious cornbread alone.

1	tablespoon olive oil
1	tablespoon butter
1	large yellow onion, peeled and chopped
1	green or red bell pepper, seeded, ribs removed, and chopped
1	medium jalapeño chile pepper, chopped (wear plastic gloves when handling)
1	tube (16 ounces) soy sausage
1	cup cornmeal
½	teaspoon salt
½	teaspoon baking soda
1	can (15 ounces) cream-style corn
1	cup plain soy milk
2	eggs, beaten
1	cup (4 ounces) shredded sharp Cheddar cheese

Preheat the oven to 350 degrees. Grease an 8-inch baking pan with shortening.

Heat the oil and butter in a medium skillet over medium-high heat. Add the onion, bell pepper, and chile pepper and sauté for 10 minutes, or until softened. Add the soy sausage, breaking it into small pieces with a fork. Remove the pan from the heat and set aside to cool.

Sift the cornmeal, salt, and baking soda into a large bowl. Add the corn, soy milk, eggs, and cheese and mix well. Add the soy sausage mixture and mix well. Scrape the batter into the prepared baking pan.

Bake for 30 minutes, or until a knife tip inserted in the center comes out clean.

LIGHT LEMON POUND CAKE

MAKES 8 TO 10 SERVINGS

This pound cake is wonderful topped with fresh fruit, toasted nuts, or a drizzle of chocolate and whipped cream.

POUND CAKE

4	ounces soft, silken tofu, drained
2	eggs, separated
2	tablespoons freshly squeezed lemon juice
1	cup sugar
¼	cup butter, softened
1½	cups unbleached white or all-purpose flour
1	teaspoon baking powder
½	teaspoon salt
	Zest of I lemon
3	tablespoons water

GLAZE

½	cup confectioners' sugar
	Juice of 1 lemon

To prepare the pound cake: Preheat the oven to 350 degrees. Lightly grease an 8-inch loaf pan with butter or coat lightly with cooking spray.

Place the tofu, egg yolks, and lemon juice in a large bowl. Beat with an electric mixer on medium speed to blend. Add the sugar and butter. Beat until creamy. Add the flour, baking powder, salt, and lemon zest. Blend until smooth. With the electric mixer, beat the egg whites and water in a separate bowl until soft peaks form. Gently fold the egg whites into the flour mixture. Spoon the batter into the prepared loaf pan and smooth it out evenly.

Bake for 1 hour. Cool completely in the pan on a rack. Run a sharp knife around the edge of the pan to loosen the loaf. Remove the loaf from the pan and place on a serving plate.

To prepare the glaze: Combine the confectioners' sugar and lemon juice in a medium bowl until well-blended. Spread the glaze over top of the loaf.

NO MOO CAKE

There are no dairy products in this cake, making it the perfect dessert for vegans.

CAKE

1½	cups whole wheat pastry flour or all-purpose flour
1	cup sugar
¼	cup unsweetened cocoa powder
1	teaspoon baking soda
½	teaspoon salt
1	cup water
⅓	cup vegetable oil
1	teaspoon white vinegar
1	teaspoon vanilla extract

FROSTING

1	cup confectioners' sugar
¼	cup unsweetened cocoa powder
2½	tablespoons plain soy milk
2	tablespoons soy margarine, softened
2	tablespoons soft, silken tofu, drained and mashed

To prepare the cake: Preheat the oven to 350 degrees. Lightly grease an 8-inch baking pan with butter or coat lightly with cooking spray. Combine the flour, sugar, cocoa powder, baking soda, and salt in a large bowl until well-blended. Add the water, oil, vinegar, and vanilla extract and stir until smoothly blended. Pour the batter into the prepared pan.

Bake for 35 to 40 minutes, or until a toothpick inserted in the center of the cake comes out clean. Cool completely in the pan on a rack. Run a sharp knife around the edge of the pan to loosen the cake. Invert the cake onto a serving plate. Cool completely.

To prepare the frosting: Combine all ingredients in a food processor. Process until smooth. Spread on the cooled cake.

EASY PIECRUST

MAKES 2 (9-INCH) PIECRUSTS

I love this piecrust because you don't have to roll it out. It's perfect for Collard Greens Quiche (page 208). Allowing the crust to chill before filling it or baking it makes it deliciously flaky. For pies with an uncooked filling, prick the bottom and sides of the crust with a fork and bake the crust at 400 degrees for 10 minutes. Cool completely before filling.

  1½   cups unbleached white flour
   ¼   cup + 2 tablespoons butter
   2   tablespoons sesame seeds
 1–2   tablespoons ice water, as needed
   2   tablespoons white vinegar

Coat two 9-inch pie pans with cooking spray. Set aside.

Place the flour, butter, and sesame seeds in a food processor. Process until the mixture resembles a coarse meal. While the machine is running, add the water and vinegar, ½ tablespoon at a time, through the feeding tube. Stop the machine as soon as a dough forms in the bowl.

Remove the dough, divide it in half, and place equal amounts in each of the prepared pie pans. Press the dough out to cover the bottom, sides, and rims of the pans. Make a decorative design around the rim by pressing the tines of a fork into the dough. Refrigerate the piecrusts for 30 minutes before filling or baking, or wrap the pie pans tightly and freeze for later use.

WHOLE WHEAT PIECRUST

MAKES 2 (9-INCH) PIECRUSTS

Whole wheat flour is an excellent source of complex carbohydrates. It also contains B vitamins, calcium, iron, magnesium, phosphorus, potassium, zinc, and other trace elements, and minimal amounts of sodium. It's nice to know that you can eat your cake (or pie) and get a large serving of vitamins, too, when you use wheat flour!

3	cups whole wheat pastry flour
1	teaspoon salt
1½	cups shortening
1	tablespoon white vinegar
1	egg
¼	cup ice water

Sift the flour and salt into a large bowl. Cut in the shortening with a pastry blender or fork.

Combine the vinegar and the egg in a small bowl. Slowly add the ice water and the egg mixture, 1 to 2 tablespoons at a time, to the flour mixture. Mix the ingredients together to form a soft dough. Work with the pastry gently to prevent the dough from becoming tough. Divide the dough in half and form into 2 balls. Wrap them in plastic wrap and freeze for later use or refrigerate for 1 to 2 hours before rolling out into a piecrust.

BEAN PIE

This recipe was inspired by the unusual creamy pies sold by Black Muslims in restaurants and on the streets of many African-American communities. This is a "pantry" pie because you can easily keep the ingredients on hand.

1	can (15 ounces) pinto beans, rinsed and drained
2	eggs
1	cup vanilla-flavored soy milk
⅔	cup sugar
¾	teaspoon salt
¼	teaspoon ground cinnamon
¼	teaspoon ground ginger
¼	teaspoon freshly grated nutmeg
¼	teaspoon ground cloves
1	Whole Wheat Piecrust (page 219) or 1 (9-inch) prepared whole wheat pie crust

Preheat the oven to 425 degrees.

Mash the beans in a bowl with a fork. With an electric mixer on low speed, beat the eggs and soy milk together in a large bowl until well-blended. Add the beans, sugar, salt, cinnamon, ginger, nutmeg, and cloves and mix well.

Prick the bottom and sides of the piecrust with a fork.

Pour the bean mixture into the crust. Bake for 15 minutes. Reduce the oven temperature to 350 degrees and rotate the pie in the oven. Bake for an additional 35 minutes, or until a knife tip inserted in the center of the pie comes out clean. Cool completely in the pan on a rack.

NEW-STYLE SWEET POTATO PIE

MAKES 8 SERVINGS

Sweet potatoes in every possible form are integral to African-American culinary history. This pie uses healthier ingredients than most desserts. Baking the potatoes before making the filling deepens their flavor.

3	medium sweet potatoes
½	cup egg substitute (equal to 2 eggs)
½	cup sugar
½	teaspoon freshly grated nutmeg
½	teaspoon ground cinnamon
½	teaspoon ground cloves
½	teaspoon ground ginger
1½	cups whole vanilla-flavored soy milk
1	unbaked Easy Piecrust (page 218) or 1 (9-inch) prepared piecrust
⅓	cup pecan pieces

Preheat the oven to 400 degrees. Line a baking sheet with foil.

Prick the sweet potatoes with a fork in several places and place them on the prepared baking sheet. Bake for 40 minutes, or until fork-tender. Allow the potatoes to cool.

Reduce the oven temperature to 350 degrees.

When cool enough to handle, cut the potatoes in half and scoop out the flesh into a large bowl. Add the egg substitute, sugar, nutmeg, cinnamon, cloves, and ginger. With an electric mixer on medium speed, mix until smooth. Add the soy milk and mix well. Place the mixture in the pie crust. Sprinkle the pecan pieces over the top.

Bake for 40 minutes, or until the pie is firm and set.

MENUS

If you're wondering about how to put the recipes in this book together to form a complete meal, wonder no more! I've come up with 14 combinations I'm sure you'll enjoy. There are breakfasts, snacks, and quick meals, as well as holiday offerings for Kwanzaa, Christmas, Thanksgiving, and other occasions. Take your pick, mix and match, give them a try. I think you'll agree that an Ethnic Vegetarian meal is truly a celebration!

Power Breakfast
Cucumber Power Drink, page 92
Cornmeal Pancakes, page 182
Fresh fruit

Quick Morning Pick-Me-Up
Seminole Orange Drink, page 119
Liberian Pineapple Nut Bread, page 50

Southern-Style Supper
Black Bean Chili, page 205
Sweet Potatoes with Peanuts à la Carver, page 178
Big Easy Spinach and Roasted Pepper Salad, page 131

Fast African Feast
Senegalase Tofu, page 46
Yellow Rice, page 43
North African Orange Salad, page 12

Simple Supper
Olive and Pasta Salad, page 128
Baked Apples, page 117

Elegant Lunch
Southwestern Tortilla Soup, page 204
Collard Greens Quiche, page 208
East African Fried Okra, page 34
Creole Pralines, page 155

Company's Coming

Corn Cakes with Texas Caviar, page 198
Portobello Mushrooms with
Parmesan Rice Timbales, page 212
Green Bean and Sesame Salad, page 200
Spoon Bread, page 191
No Moo Cake, page 217

Caribbean-Style Family Reunion Barbecue

Jerk Tofu, page 78
Jerk-Grilled Vegetables, page 77
Grilled Greens, page 209
Coleslaw, page 160
Crescent City Potato Salad, page 130
Barbecued Beans, page 170
Island Bread Pudding, page 85

Thanksgiving Dinner

Pumpkin Soup, page 102
Smothered Chicken Seitan
with Veggie Gravy, page 176
Baked Tomatoes and Onions
with Cornbread Stuffing, page 186
Garlic Mashed Potatoes
with Broccoli Coulis, page 150
Macaroni and Cheese, page 173
Kenyan-Style Mixed Greens, page 21
Cranberry Sauce, page 97
Aunt Florine's Jalapeño Cornbread, page 215
New-Style Sweet Potato Pie, page 221

Christmas Dinner

Mango Eggnog, page 92
Crudités with Jezebel Sauce, page 126
Caribbean Sweet Potato Bisque, page 71
Creole Rice Cakes with Spicy Tomato Sauce, page 152
Plantain Patties, page 74
Bean Pie, page 220

Kwanzaa Karamu Feast

Bean Scoops, page 8
Egyptian Chickpea Sesame Spread, page 6
Ethnic-Style Jambalaya, page 142
Tanzanian Baked Bananas, page 54

New Years Day Dinner

Black Bean and Plantain Fritters, page 72
Marinated Onions, page 68
Hopping John, page 171
Tanzanian Fried Cabbage, page 20
Light Lemon Pound Cake, page 216

New Orleans-Style Football Buffet

Okra Gumbo, page 134
Portobella Muffuletta, page 143
Dirty Rice, page 149
Ethnic-Style Gingerbread, page 192

Snacks

Trail Mix, page 97
Sunflower Seed Snacks, page 100
Mohawk Potato Chips, page 98

NUTRITION AND HEALTH

IF THERE'S ONE "GOLDEN RULE" ABOUT SEEKING
a vegetarian lifestyle, it's that there is no "right" type of vegetarian, only the type that is right for you. And even that
may change. As you learn more about being a vegetarian, you
may decide to eliminate some foods and embrace others.
You may start out as an ethnic or semi-vegetarian and gradually become a vegan. The important thing to keep in mind
during this journey is that you are taking the right steps toward a healthier future. To help you choose the path that works
best for you, the following sections discuss the different types

of vegetarianism and the basic nutrition information every vegetarian should know.

TYPES OF VEGETARIANS

Whether you choose to avoid meat and dairy of any kind, or filter certain kinds of these foods into your diet, you're likely to find that a vegetarian menu provides so many options there's very little risk of every growing bored. The key is to make your own choices based on your personal dietary needs and belief system. The following descriptions will help you decide what works for you.

- **ETHNIC VEGETARIAN:** Largely a vegetable- and grain-based diet, this type of vegetarianism includes dairy products and eggs and occasionally incorporates chicken or fish but basically no red meat. It's a diet based upon cultural heritage and the desire for a healthier lifestyle.

- **SEMI-VEGETARIAN:** Largely vegetable- and grain-based, this form includes dairy products, eggs, chicken, and fish, and occasionally, red meat.

- **LACTO-OVO VEGETARIAN:** This description fits most people who define themselves as vegetarians and includes vegetables, fruits, grains, eggs, and dairy products. It excludes meat, chicken, and fish.

- **LACTO-VEGETARIAN:** This form of vegetarianism includes vegetables, fruits, grains, and dairy products, including cheese, yogurt, and butter. It excludes eggs, meat, chicken, and fish.

- **OVO-VEGETARIANS:** Those embracing this type eat vegetables, fruits, grains, and eggs. They do not eat meat, chicken, fish, or dairy products.

- **VEGANS** (*pronounced VEE-guns*): Also known as strict, or pure, vegetarians, vegans eat vegetables, fruits, and grains. They do not eat meat, chicken, fish, dairy products, or any products produced by living creatures, such as honey.

- **FRUITARIANS:** This diet consists of all fruits including those that are commonly considered vegetables, such as avocados, tomatoes, zucchini, and eggplant. It also includes seeds, grains, and nuts. No animal products (except honey) or vegetables are eaten. This diet is difficult for many to maintain indefinitely and is not recommended for children.

- **RAW FOODS DIET:** This consists primarily of uncooked foods, mainly vegetables, fruits, nuts, seeds, sprouted grains, and beans. The reason behind eating foods in their raw state is that cooking can destroy some of their nutrients. This diet is not recommended for children because cooked food is easier to digest. Cooking also helps eliminate harmful bacteria and germs.

- **MACROBIOTIC DIET:** This type combines some of the principles of Buddhism and the Chinese philosophy of yin and yang, or balance in life. This category of vegetarians practices a diet more commonly found in Asia. Some of the foods consumed on this diet are vegetables; legumes; fruits; whole grains; root vegetables such as daikon; sea vegetables such as wakame, kelp, nori, and arame; and Asian condiments like miso. It excludes all animal products; dairy; eggs; refined sugars; certain vegetables (called nightshade vegetables) such as potatoes, tomatoes, eggplant, and green peppers; and tropical fruits. This regimen focuses heavily on the quality of the food, its preparation, and on portion sizes to promote harmony and balance. Some followers of this diet also believe it is effective for curing illnesses.

NUTRITION BASICS FOR VEGETARIANS

Overall, vegetarian diets are extremely healthy when followed properly. They have been tested and approved time and time again by medical experts, including the American Dietetic Association, as meeting all nutritional needs. But with so many types of vegetarian diets available, how can you be sure you're really getting everything you need? Most experts advise new vegetarians to remember one word: variety. If you eat a reasonable variety of whole grains, fruits, vegetables, sea vegetables, potatoes, corn, peas, greens, beans, and legumes, you can be confident you're getting the nutrients you need for good health.

Along the same lines, it's important to remember that eliminating meat from your diet doesn't mean that you now have additional daily calories that you can use to consume unhealthy foods. Becoming a vegetarian means that you must continue to monitor the amounts of sweets and high-fat foods that you eat.

As you learn more about the food choices you make, the following information can help you understand how a vegetarian diet can provide the nutrients that will lead to better health.

PROTEIN: The proteins that are found in vegetable sources such as whole grains, legumes, nuts, and seeds provide the nutrients necessary to build muscle, skin, connective tissues, and almost every other body part, as long as the sources of protein are varied and caloric intake is high enough to meet energy needs. Contrary to the old views on vegetarian diets, it is not necessary to mix a number of vegetable proteins within a given meal to get your daily protein requirement. And while protein is naturally found in most plant foods, it's easy to get even more into your diet. Look for commercially prepared protein-packed foods made from soy, tofu, and wheat glutens that are flavored to taste like every type of meat, from beef and chicken to pork sausages. If you rely on convenience foods, you can even find protein-packed frozen dinners for vegetarians in most larger grocery stores.

IRON: This mineral is mostly found in hemaglobin, the protein in red blood cells that transports oxygen through the bloodstream. Vegetarians get their iron from leafy greens, whole grains, soybeans, tofu, members of the cabbage family, and root vegetables. Eating foods high in vitamin C such as citrus fruits, black currants, guavas, berries, broccoli, and bell peppers will help your body absorb iron.

VITAMIN B_{12}: This vitamin maintains the nervous system and helps with the production of red blood cells. Eating the required daily amounts of dairy

(continued on page 232)

THE VEGETARIAN DIET PYRAMID

Vegetarian diets have been shown in studies to be helpful in reducing the incidence of high blood pressure and coronary artery disease and in lowering cholesterol levels.

Since African-Americans statistically suffer in greater numbers from these diseases, a vegetarian diet is a wise lifestyle choice for them or anyone at risk for these diseases.

The Vegetarian Diet Pyramid is a valuable reference that will help you determine the amounts of dairy products, whole grains, seeds, nuts, legumes, plant oils, fruits, and vegetables you will need to maintain proper nutrition. Notice that paramount to maintaining good health is daily physical activity, which makes up the base of the pyramid.

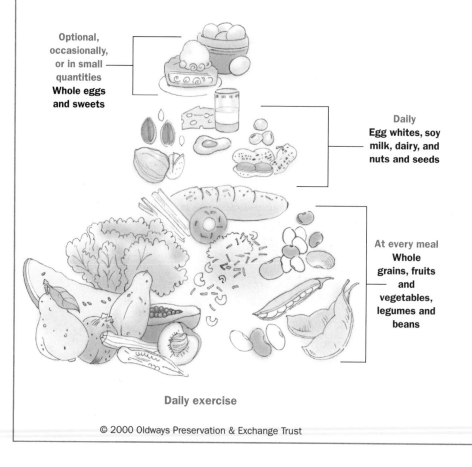

Optional, occasionally, or in small quantities
Whole eggs and sweets

Daily
Egg whites, soy milk, dairy, and nuts and seeds

At every meal
Whole grains, fruits and vegetables, legumes and beans

Daily exercise

© 2000 Oldways Preservation & Exchange Trust

Fruits. Include fruit at every meal. A serving equals $1/2$ cup of chopped raw fruit, $1/2$ cup of canned fruit, 1 medium-size piece of fruit, $1/4$ cup of dried fruit, or $3/4$ cup of juice.

Vegetables. Vegetables should also be eaten at every meal. A serving equals 1 cup of raw, leafy vegetables or $1/2$ cup of cooked or chopped raw vegetables.

Whole grains. Include grains at each meal. Choose from foods such as oats, wheat, whole grain bread, barley, couscous, noodles, whole wheat pasta, or corn. A serving equals 1 slice of bread; 1 ounce of ready-to-eat cereal; $1/2$ cup of cooked cereal; $1/2$ cup of cooked rice, pasta, or other grain; or $1/2$ bagel.

Legumes and beans. Eat these foods at every meal, including soy beans or peanuts, lentils, peas, tofu, kidney beans, navy beans, pinto beans, split peas, lima beans, chickpeas, black beans, red beans, and textured vegetable protein. A serving equals 1 to $1^1/2$ cups of cooked, dried beans.

Nuts and seeds. Choose from a wide variety, including Brazil nuts, almonds, cashews, hazelnuts, macadamia nuts, pine nuts, pistachios, sesame seeds, and pumpkin seeds. These can be included daily.

Egg whites, soy milk, and dairy. Have a daily serving of egg whites and dairy or soy cheese, yogurt, or milk.

Plant oils. Choose from among avocado, canola, corn, olive, soybean, safflower, peanut, and other nut and seed oils for your daily serving.

Whole eggs and sweets. Have small quantities of items such as ice cream, cake, cookies, eggs, pie, and other standard dessert fare, or eat them only occasionally. It's best to choose whole, unrefined foods as often as possible and minimize your intake of highly sweetened, fatty, and heavily refined foods.

products should provide sufficient amounts of B_{12}. Vegetarians who don't eat dairy products should take B_{12} supplements.

VITAMIN D: Your body uses vitamin D to help absorb calcium, which builds healthy teeth and bones and aids in the functions of the muscles and nervous system. Vitamin D is present in fortified milk and synthesized by exposure to adequate sunlight. Vegetarians who don't eat dairy products need to take vitamin D supplements, especially during the winter months, when many people have less exposure to vitamin D from sunlight.

CALCIUM: Consuming enough calcium for a healthy diet does not require the consumption of dairy products. Many people are lactose intolerant, making dairy products impossible to digest without discomfort. Or, you may decide to become an ovo-vegetarian, fruitarian, or a vegan, types of vegetarians that do not consume dairy products.

Fortunately, many products from juices to rice are fortified with calcium. There are also a number of tasty and nutritious substitutions for many dairy products, most of which are made from soy or fortified tofu, such as soy-based versions of milk, butter, mayonnaise, sour cream, and cheese. Best of all, they taste good, and they're good for you.

Other good sources of calcium include bok choy and beans. Dark green leafy vegetables such as collard and mustard greens, kale, turnip greens, and broccoli are also excellent sources of calcium. While $\frac{1}{2}$ cup of milk has approximately 138 milligrams of calcium, $\frac{1}{2}$ cup of tofu made with calcium has 250 milligrams, $\frac{1}{2}$ cup of raw kale has 45 milligrams, and $\frac{1}{2}$ cup of collards has 26 milligrams. Studies have shown that vegetarians absorb and retain more calcium from foods than nonvegetarians do. There are also a number of dietary supplements that will provide the additional calcium and vitamin B_{12} you may need if you decide to become a vegan. Check with your doctor before beginning a regimen of dietary supplements.

WATER: Here's some important advice that applies to everyone, vegetarian or not. Aim for six to eight 8-ounce glasses of water per day, or half your body weight in ounces.

FIBER: Fiber is the indigestible part of plants that helps protect against many diseases. And, not surprisingly, vegetarians usually get plenty of fiber in their diets from the fruits and vegetables they eat. But to achieve good health, many experts also recommend boosting intake of whole grains and eliminating white flours that are found in most pastas, breads, and biscuits.

The good news is that it is fairly easy to find these items made with nutritional flours such as wheat, rye, and soy. It just takes a quick look at package labels to find what you're looking for. Most of the recipes in this book that use flour call for whole wheat flour first, with an option for all-purpose flour. Both will work well, but I prefer to use the whole wheat variety for better nutrition.

THE ROAD TO WELLNESS

Becoming a vegetarian requires some lifestyle adjustments that are extremely beneficial to your health. It's fine to start this new adjustment slowly, one food product or recipe at a time, as you eliminate the meat dishes and processed foods that you ate in the past. Learn as much as you can about being a vegetarian so that you feel comfortable about your food choices when shopping for groceries or dining out in restaurants. A delicious meal is a wonderful thing, especially when you know that what you're eating is not only good, it's good for you.

A key to success is preparation. This book is designed to provide you with the information you'll need to prepare you to be the type of vegetarian you want to be. A long journey begins with a single step. Consider your decision to become a vegetarian the first step on the road to well-being.

THE ETHNIC VEGETARIAN KITCHEN

THIS SECTION IS A GUIDE TO STOCKING AN ETHNIC vegetarian kitchen, from the equipment you'll find useful in preparing the recipes to the ingredients you'll need on hand in your pantry . I'm sure you'll be pleasantly surprised to find that you won't have to run out and buy dozens of new gadgets or a mountain of new ingredients. You may already have many of the items I recommend.

If you're trying a new ingredient for the first time, you might want to start out by buying the smallest quantity available. Another way to "test drive" an unfamiliar ingredient is to sample it at a restaurant. These methods allow you to experiment with foods and flavorings that may be unfamiliar to you.

BASIC EQUIPMENT

Here's a rundown of the equipment that I use the most in ethnic vegetarian cooking.

FOOD PROCESSOR: You may want to invest in a large, sturdy food processor if you don't have one already. I find that I use my food processor every day. It's great for everything from chopping vegetables to making piecrust dough. The food processor is a time- and labor-saving device. If possible, buy one with a large bowl and a heavy-duty motor.

HANDHELD IMMERSION BLENDER: This is extremely useful for pureeing soups, making dressings, and mashing vegetables. As the name implies, you can immerse the appliance right into a pot or bowl to mix whatever you're cooking.

CAST-IRON SKILLET: Cast iron absorbs and retains heat extremely well, so it's practically indispensable for preparing vegetarian recipes. It helps foods cook quickly and evenly.

And cast iron has come a long way, baby. You can now find cast iron that does not have to go through the long "seasoning" process that took lots of oil, high temperatures, and time, but made your grandmother's recipes taste so good. It is seasoned in the factory with vegetable oil, which is then "baked" onto the cookware with extremely high heat. Use these skillets to cook everything from sauces to stews to cornbread beautifully and evenly.

LARGE, HEAVY-BOTTOMED SKILLET: Look for one with a tight-fitting lid. This pan will serve you well. You'll use it frequently for techniques such as stir-frying, sautéing, and frying.

LARGE, HEAVY-BOTTOMED SOUP POT: Again, try to find one with a tight-fitting lid. These durable pots come in handy for cooking pasta as well as big-batch items like soups and stews.

LARGE COLANDER: You'll use this often for draining foods such as pasta and canned beans and vegetables.

PANTRY STAPLES

Just because you are about to embark on an exciting new culinary adventure doesn't mean that you have to completely surrender your pantry to new ingredients. Add new ingredients one recipe and one trip to the grocery store at a time. Find recipes that you'd like to try, note the ingredients you don't have, and purchase those first. As you become more familiar with the ingredients necessary for vegetarian cooking, your pantry will gradually expand.

Here is a comprehensive grocery list of pantry and refrigerator/freezer items called for in many of the recipes in this cookbook, followed by a section that identifies various essential vegetarian ingredients and their uses. Some prepared foods—things like stocks, Italian seasoning, garlic mayonnaise, vegetarian Worcestershire sauce, and seitan—can be made at home rather than purchased ready made. I've included my own recipes for these foods beginning on page 253.

OILS

Canola oil
Cooking spray
Olive oil, both extra virgin and virgin
Peanut oil
Shortening
Sunflower seed oil
Walnut oil

SWEETENERS

Brown sugar, both dark and light
Confectioners' sugar
Honey
Maple sugar or maple syrup
Molasses
Sugar

BAKING INGREDIENTS

All-purpose flour
Arrowroot flour
Baking powder

Baking soda
Bread crumbs
Cocoa, unsweetened
Cornstarch
Cornmeal
Self-rising flour
Whole wheat flours, including
    Whole wheat pastry flour and
    Whole wheat gluten flour

DAIRY PRODUCTS

Butter, both salted and unsalted
Buttermilk
Cheeses, including Cheddar and Swiss
Cream, both heavy and light
Cream cheese
Eggs
Half-and-half
Milk, whole
Sour cream
Yogurt, plain

SOY PRODUCTS

Soy cream cheese
Soy ground beef
Soy sausage, including
    Italian-style links
Soy margarine
Soy milk, both plain and
    vanilla-flavored
Soy yogurt, vanilla
Tofu, silken, both firm and soft
Vegetable protein flakes
    (soy flakes)

Allspice

Basil

Bay leaves

Black pepper

Cajun seasoning

Capers

Cardamom pods

Cayenne pepper

Celery seed

Chili powder

Cilantro

Cinnamon

Cloves

Coriander

Cream of tartar

Cumin

Curry powder

Dry mustard

Garlic powder

Ginger

Italian seasoning

Jerk seasoning

Marjoram

Mint

Nutmeg

Onion powder

Oregano

Paprika

Parsley, flat leaf

Peppercorns

Poultry seasoning

Red-pepper flakes

Rosemary

Rum-flavored extract

Saffron

Sage
Sea salt
Tarragon
Thyme
Turmeric
White pepper
Vanilla extract
Yellow mustard seeds

DRIED FRUITS, NUTS, AND SEEDS

Almonds, roasted
Apples, dried
Apricots, dried
Coconut, unsweetened, shredded
Cranberries, dried
Fruit mix, dried
Hazelnuts
Peanuts, green
Peanuts, unsalted, roasted
Pecans
Pine nuts
Pumpkin seeds
Raisins
Sesame seeds
Sunflower seeds
Walnuts

CONDIMENTS

Apple cider vinegar
Apple jelly
Balsamic vinegar
Barbecue sauce
Horseradish
Hot-pepper sauce

Ketchup

Malt vinegar

Marmalade, orange

Mayonnaise

Mustard, including Dijon, spicy,
    and stone ground

Pickapeppa sauce

Preserves, peach

Soy sauce

Sweet pickle relish

Vinegar, including red wine, rice wine,
    white and white wine

Wine, including dry red
    and dry white

Worcestershire sauce, vegetarian

CANNED PRODUCTS

Apples, sliced (20-ounce cans)

Artichoke hearts ($6\frac{1}{2}$-ounce cans)

Baked beans (20-ounce cans)

Black beans (15-ounce cans)

Black-eyed peas (15-ounce cans)

Chickpeas (15-ounce cans)

Chipotle peppers (15-ounce cans)

Coconut milk, both sweetened and
    unsweetened (14-ounce cans)

Corn, both cream-style and
    whole kernel (15-ounce cans)

Dill pickles, sliced (16-ounce jars)

Green beans (15-ounce cans)

Hominy (15-ounce cans)

Evaporated milk (12-ounce cans)

Kidney beans (15-ounce cans)

Olives, both black pitted and green
    pimiento-stuffed (16-ounce jars)

Onions, fried (6-ounce cans)
Pickled cauliflower and sweet peppers
    (16-ounce jars)
Pineapple, crushed (15-ounce cans)
Pinto beans (15-ounce cans)
Pumpkin (15-ounce cans)
Roasted red bell peppers (19-ounce jars)
Soup, cream of mushroom (10-ounce cans)
Sweet potatoes (15-ounce cans)
Salsa (16-ounce jars)
Tomatoes, both paste and sauce
    (8-ounce cans)
Tomatoes, diced both plain (14- and 28-ounce
    cans) and with green chilies (10-ounce cans)
Tomatoes, peeled whole
    (15-, 20-, and 28-ounce cans)
Tomatoes, stewed (15-ounce cans)
Vegetable broth (14-ounce cans)

GRAIN PRODUCTS, PASTA, AND DRIED BEANS

Couscous
Cream of wheat (not instant)
Elbow macaroni
Hominy grits (not quick-cooking)
Lentils
Lima beans
Melba toast
Navy beans
Oats, old-fashioned rolled
Peanut butter, both chunky and smooth
Pearl barley
Penne pasta
Pigeon peas
Pita bread
Red beans

Rice, including basmati, long-grain, and
short-grain white
Seitan, including beef-flavored and
chicken-flavored
Tortillas, both corn and flour
Vermicelli

Black-eyed peas
Collard greens
Corn
Green beans
Green peas
Mustard greens
Okra
Piecrusts, 9-inch
Spinach
Turnip greens
Vegetables, mixed

INGREDIENT GUIDE

Now that you have your grocery list in hand, it may help you to know a little
more about the foods you'll be cooking with. Below are brief definitions and
descriptions of some of the foods and products used in this book.

GREENS

"A mess of greens" used to be the centerpiece of many of my ancestors'
meals. A variety of greens were seasoned and cooked for hours. The "pot
liquor," or cooking liquid, was prized for pouring over a piece of cornbread
or for sipping like a soup. Today, greens are quickly blanched and then
cooked for minutes rather than hours, to retain their nutrients. Even though

it doesn't cook as long, the flavorful pot liquor is still as delicious today as it was then. The more delicate greens, such as spinach and Swiss chard, should be used within 1 to 2 days of purchase. The heartier greens will keep for a few days longer. Here's a rundown of the greens that I use the most. For instructions on preparing greens, see page 252.

DANDELION GREENS: My ancestors picked these greens straight out of the yard and cooked them in combination with other greens. Because of the large amounts of chemicals that are used today, it isn't advisable to pick wild dandelion greens. These "weed" greens are best purchased commercially.

KALE AND COLLARD GREENS: Kale has distinctive curly leaves or flat leaves that have thick ribs branching through them. Collard greens are a relative of kale. Both have a strong taste and are high in vitamin A. Cut the leaves away from the tough stems and discard the stems. Kale and collards take longer to cook than most greens, but they hold their volume better.

MUSTARD GREENS: These have crinkled leaves, tough stems and ribs, and a peppery, sharp, mustard flavor. Remove the stems and ribs unless the greens are young and tender.

SPINACH: The leaves of this green are tender and delicious and can be used raw in salads or cooked in a variety of ways.

SWISS CHARD: A member of the beet family, Swiss chard has large green leaves with thick white ribs running through them. Cut the leaves away from the stems, chop the stems, and cook them with the leaves. These greens are often used interchangeably with spinach, but they have a stronger, more distinctive taste.

TURNIP GREENS: These flavorful greens have crinkled leaves and a rough texture. They lend themselves perfectly to soups and stews, because the flavor becomes deeper and more complex as the leaves cook.

GRAINS, FLOUR, AND MEAL

A basic understanding of grains is necessary to cook ethnic vegetarian meals. Some of the proteins they contain will replace the proteins you may have formerly derived from eating meat. Barley, buckwheat, corn, cornmeal, flaxseed, oats, oat bran, quinoa, rice, teff, and wheat flour are used in the recipes in this book. Here's a little more about them. Each grain is unique, so it's best to follow package or recipe directions when preparing them.

BARLEY: This is one of the oldest grains ever cultivated. Pearl barley is the most common modern variety available. The outer husk and part of the bran layer of the kernels is removed to shorten cooking time. It contains vitamins B_1 and B_3 as well as potassium.

CORN: This is also a grain, though we mostly eat it as a vegetable. When whole kernel corn is added to breads, it adds a crunchy texture and naturally sweet flavor. It is one of the most versatile grains in that it can be added to main or side dishes and paired with legumes. For instructions on preparing corn, see page 251.

CORNMEAL: Made from dried corn kernels that have been ground, cornmeal is available in both degerminated and whole grain forms. In the degerminated form, both the germ and bran have been removed. This is the most common type found in grocery stores. Stone ground whole grain cornmeal is less common but may be found in specialty or health food stores or at a local mill. The retained germ and bran give it more flavor, texture, and fiber.

OATS: The oats that are cooked and eaten in a common breakfast (oatmeal) are actually steamed and flattened hulled oat kernels (groats). Three varieties are available. They are regular (old-fashioned), quick-cooking, and instant. Although regular and quick-cooking oatmeal are often interchangeable, be careful not to substitute when a recipe calls for a specific one. Doing so may cause unexpected results because each variety has a different absorption rate. Oats have fiber, phosphorus, vitamin B_6, and magnesium.

OAT BRAN: The crushed husks of the oat kernels, oat bran is often used as a cooking and baking ingredient. It is easier to digest than wheat bran and is an excellent source of soluble fiber.

RICE: Several varieties of rice are used in the recipes in this cookbook. Long-grain rice is used in recipes for casseroles, soups, and salads. Short-grain rice, such as arborio, is used in the recipes that call for a sweet, sticky rice, such as rice puddings, risotto, and sushi. Brown rice makes a lovely accompaniment, especially when the precooked or quick-cooking versions are used. Brown rice usually takes 40 to 50 minutes to cook. Wild rice is really a seed from a North American aquatic grass. It takes at least 40 minutes to cook, but it is also available precooked.

WHEAT FLOUR: Wheat flour, including all-purpose flour and whole wheat pastry flour, is the flour of choice in the recipes in this book. Wheat flour is found in several different forms, including these:

All-purpose flour is milled from hard wheat cultivated in the winter or a blend of hard and soft winter wheat. Acceptable results are obtained when this flour is used in a wide range of baked products.

Bread flour is milled from hard winter wheat, hard spring wheat, or a combination of the two. Yeast breads require this flour because of its special gluten structure.

Cake flour is milled from soft wheat. The gluten it contains is less dense, resulting in tender-textured cakes with more volume.

Quick-mixing flour is an instant, all-purpose flour that disperses easily in cold liquids. It is ideal for batters, sauces, and smooth gravies.

Spelt flour is one of the most ancient of cultivated grains. Its use has been traced back more than 7,000 years. Spelt is high in fiber and easy to digest and is usually recommended for people who have gluten intolerances or wheat allergies.

Whole wheat flour is made from a combination of ground whole wheat kernels of winter wheat and the hard wheat cultivated in the spring. It contains many beneficial nutrients of whole wheat berries.

WHEAT BERRIES: These are the hulled whole grain kernels of wheat that still have the germ and the bran. When cooked, they can be a substitute for rice in salads and other side dishes. They provide high levels of B vitamins, complex carbohydrates, and vitamin E.

WHEAT BRAN: This is the hard outer layer of the wheat berry. It is easier to chew when cooked, but it can also be eaten in its unprocessed raw form. It is a good source of insoluble fiber.

CRACKED WHEAT: Dried whole-wheat kernels that are cracked by coarse milling, cracked wheat contains potassium, phosphorus, some iron, and vitamins B_1 and B_2.

WHEAT BULGUR: Wheat bulgur results when cooked whole wheat is dried and broken into coarse fragments. Unlike cracked wheat, it is precooked. It contains potassium, phosphorus, iron, and vitamins B_1 and B_2.

WHEAT GERM: This is the "heart" of the wheat berry. It has a high oil content and a limited shelf life in its raw form unless it is toasted. With a nutlike taste, it is delicious sprinkled over cereal or used in baked goods. It provides an excellent source of niacin, potassium, and zinc.

Legumes and pastas are staples in a vegetarian diet. They provide texture, flavor, and heartiness. Here are a few of the many varieties. For instructions on preparing beans, see page 250.

BLACK BEANS: Used in chilis, stews, and soups, these oval-shaped beans have a strong flavor and creamy texture.

BLACK-EYED PEAS: Also called cowpeas, these creamy peas with black "eyes" in the center are often paired with greens and rice. They're a popular ingredient in African and Southern recipes.

CHICKPEAS (GARBANZO BEANS): These beans are round, golden, nutty-tasting, and meaty-textured. The fresh variety takes a while to cook, but canned are an acceptable, speedier substitute.

COUSCOUS: Although it has properties similar to grains, couscous is technically a pasta. It's available in whole-grain and refined varieties, and it's the perfect "fast food," as it soaks up liquids in mere minutes to become a light and fluffy base for salads or main dishes.

KIDNEY BEANS AND RED BEANS: Kidney beans are very similar to red beans, but they are somewhat larger. They're often used in chilis, salads, and Hispanic recipes.

LENTILS: Tiny, disk-shaped, and quick-cooking, these legumes come in brown, green, and red varieties. Popular in Indian recipes, lentils have become more common in American dishes. They're used in soups, salads, stews, and pilafs and are also mashed into patties.

PINTO BEANS: Pink in color, with a creamy, mild taste, these beans are popular in Hispanic cooking. They're the perfect base for pungent spices, garlic, and peppers.

VERMICELLI: Italian for "little worms," this pasta is much thinner than spaghetti and cooks quickly, which is possibly why it is the pasta of choice in many ethnic recipes.

CHILE PEPPERS

Jalapeño and serrano chile peppers are used liberally throughout the recipes in this book. Jalapeño peppers are one of the most popular chiles, second only to the extremely hot habanero. Jalapeños are found in most bottled salsas. They're approximately 2 to 3 inches long and have a cylindrical shape tapering to a narrow, rounded end. They range in color from bright green to dark red. When red in color and fully ripened, jalapeños are a little sweeter. Removing the seeds and ribs also removes some of the "heat." Dried, smoked red jalapeños are called chipotles. Chipotles are a light brown color, have a smoky scent, and are often used in soups, stews, and salsas.

Serrano chile peppers are smaller and about five times hotter than jalapeños. They range in color from light green to red, brown, orange, and yellow as they ripen. Serranos have an elongated, cylindrical shape with a blunt end and are about $2\frac{1}{4}$ inches long. They are thin-skinned and are best when minced finely, without attempting to remove the seeds. For details on handling chile peppers, see "Preparing Fresh Chile Peppers" on page 251.

MUSHROOMS

Mushrooms come in several varieties, from small to large and fresh to dried, and they provide a rich, flavorful texture to vegetarian dishes. The broth from dried mushrooms provides a wonderful flavor base for sauces, stews, and soups. Mushrooms are largely composed of water, so they lose volume and size as they cook. They also absorb fat, so cooking mushrooms in a good quality oil or butter adds to the flavor of any dish. Mushrooms need to be cooked quickly, without crowding, so that they don't stew in their own juices. Use them within a day or two of purchase. Plastic bags, cellophane wrap, and plastic cartons cause mushrooms to sweat, becoming slimy and unappealing, so the best thing to do is store them loosely in the bottom of the refrigerator.

Here's a quick primer on mushrooms. For more on handling mushrooms, see page 252.

BUTTON MUSHROOMS: Most grocery stores carry this variety of mushroom. Button mushrooms range in size from tiny with a white, tightly closed cap to medium-size with visible gills under the caps. They have a pleasant flavor and are best when purchased with unblemished caps.

CHANTERELLES: This type of mushroom has a mild flavor and adds a gentle perfume to a dish. It has a flared, open shape, similar to a trumpet.

ENOKI: Pronounced "e-NOH-kee," these are commonly found in Japanese dishes and are often used as a garnish. They have a light, mild flavor, and long stems with small, button-shaped tops.

MOREL: Pronounced "moh-REL," this type of mushroom has dark brown spongy caps that hold a rich flavor. Sometimes dirt and insects are hidden in the caps, so wipe them with a damp cloth or paper towel to remove any debris.

PORCINI: These bun-shaped mushrooms are usually large in size. They have a rich, meaty, spongy texture underneath the cap that is usually scraped away. The stem is usually slightly tough and needs to be trimmed before use or chopped finely before it's added to a recipe.

SOY FOODS

Many vegetarians rely heavily on soy products to provide them with adequate protein in their diets. Here are a few of the mainstays.

SOYBEANS: A great source of protein, iron, and vitamin E, these beans are the basis for a number of soy products. Soybeans have a bland taste, but they absorb seasonings and spices very well.

SOY CHEESE: An alternative to dairy cheese and similar in taste, soy cheese is made from soy milk and/or often contains small amounts of casein, a milk product that makes cheese melt. Vegans and people who are lactose intolerant might want to try soy cheese that doesn't contain casein. Soy cheese is high in fat, but it's cholesterol-free.

SOY MILK: This rich-textured milk is made from a blend of soybeans and water and comes in several flavorful varieties, including vanilla, chocolate, and hazelnut. It also comes in unflavored and "lite" varieties. Soy milk provides more than 3 grams of fiber per cup.

SOY YOGURT: This alternative to dairy yogurt is lactose- and cholesterol-free because it is made from cultured soy milk. Available in a variety of flavors, soy yogurt is perfect for vegans and anyone who is lactose intolerant.

TOFU: Also known as soybean curd and most commonly used in Asian recipes, tofu has a mild taste and many uses, from stir-fries to desserts.

Because of its texture, tofu has the ability to absorb the flavors in which it's immersed—in essence, it "mimics" other flavors. It is available in soft, firm, and extra-firm varieties. Soft is best for sauces and desserts, and the firm and extra-firm are best for cubing, skewering, or slicing into slabs or strips. Tofu is high in protein (10 grams per 4 ounces of tofu), but it is also high in fat (about 50 percent of the total calories). If this is a concern, you may want to try the many "lite" versions of tofu that are available.

MEAT SUBSTITUTES

There's no shortage of products available to help take the place of meat in vegetarian cooking. Here's a sampling of what's available.

SOY MEAT PRODUCTS: Soy sausage, Italian links, ground meat, taco meat, and a variety of hot dogs, luncheon meats, and other meat-substitute products are readily available in most grocery stores. While most of the products are acceptable meat substitutes, others are an acquired taste. Try different brands and varieties to decide which ones you prefer.

TEXTURED VEGETABLE PROTEIN (TVP): TVP is what is left after the oil is extracted from soybeans. It's sold flavored and unflavored in a variety of forms, including chunked, minced, and flaked. It has a meaty quality when reconstituted with water or broth and added to casseroles, soups, or stews.

WHEAT GLUTEN (SEITAN): Made from whole wheat flour, this meat substitute can be purchased in health food stores or made at home. (See the recipe on page 256.) Commercially packaged seitan is available plain or in chicken or beef flavors.

BASIC RECIPES AND TECHNIQUES FOR THE ETHNIC VEGETARIAN

Several of the ingredients in the pantry list beginning on page 235 are items that can be made at home. The store-bought varieties are excellent, and you'll be very pleased with the results they yield. But if you enjoy experimenting in the kitchen, try your hand at making them yourself.

First, there are two terrific starters, 1-2-3 Vegetable Broth and Rich Vegetable Broth. These are wonderful bases for all sorts of soups and stews. You can also add them to simmering vegetables for an extra boost of flavor or use them instead of water when you cook rice and other grains.

Another homemade creation is my Garlic-Tofu Mayonnaise. It's a delicious, healthy alternative to regular mayo, and it's nondairy, so it's great for vegans, ovo-vegetarians, and those who may be lactose intolerant.

Then there's Vegetarian Worcestershire Sauce. Store-bought Worcestershire sauce is terrific, but because it's made with anchovies, it doesn't fit into a vegetarian lifestyle. So I've created my own version that's the perfect alternative.

My Italian Seasoning Mix is also handy to have around. It's quick and easy to prepare—much quicker than making a special trip to the grocery store.

I've also included a recipe for seitan (SAY-tan), a food with a long history in Asia and Middle Eastern countries. Seitan is gluten that has been extracted from wheat flour. It's called "wheat meat" in some places, as the texture is similar to meat. It contains no fat, and it is high in protein. I've used several brands of commercially prepared seitan and soy meats with great success, so don't be afraid to try these wonderful time-saving products as well.

BASIC TECHNIQUES

Some of the ingredients I use frequently in this book require a little bit of preparation. The instructions below will make quick work of preparing foods such as dried beans, fresh chile peppers, corn, greens, and mushrooms. I've also provided instructions for blanching vegetables and toasting nuts and seeds.

Preparing Dried Beans

Store dried beans in a glass jar and stick a couple of dried chile peppers in with them. The chiles will keep pantry bugs from invading your beans.

To prepare dried beans, spread the beans in a single layer on a baking sheet and pick out any stones and shriveled or discolored beans. Dump the beans into a large bowl of water and swish them around. Discard any beans that float to the top. Transfer the rest of the beans to a sieve and rinse them.

Put the beans in a saucepan. Cover them with four times their volume of cold water (about 4 cups water for each cup of beans). Cover and set aside for 6 to 8 hours or overnight, until the beans have doubled in size. When one is cut open, it should be moist all the way through. Drain the beans and discard the soaking water. Cook as desired.

Keep in mind that lima beans and pinto beans do not need soaking.

To do a "quick-soak," place rinsed and sorted dried beans in a saucepan with four times their volume of cold water (about 4 cups water for each cup of beans). Bring to a boil. Reduce the heat to medium-low and simmer about 10 minutes. Cover, remove from the heat, and let stand for about 1 hour.

Preparing Fresh Chile Peppers

Always wear plastic gloves when preparing fresh chile peppers. Failure to do so will result in a burning sensation in your hands and any other part of your body you touch. Never use hot water to rinse fresh peppers. The hot water may cause fumes that will irritate your eyes and nose.

When preparing fresh chile peppers, remove the stems and seeds with your gloved fingers. You may also use a paring knife if the ribs of the pepper are thick and fleshy. Removing the seeds from the peppers retains the flavor while greatly decreasing the "heat." (Serrano chile peppers may be used whole, because the seeds are difficult to remove.) Always wash your hands thoroughly with soap and cold water when you are finished preparing the peppers. Be sure to clean any utensils or surfaces that have come in contact with the peppers.

Preparing Fresh Corn

First remove the husks and silks from each ear of corn. Rinse the ears and pat them dry. Place the small end of the ear into a large bowl to catch the milk (the sweet juices that remain).

Using a sharp knife, cut the corn away from the cob with a gentle sawing motion. Leave about one-third of the kernels attached as you slice so that the slightly tough, fibrous ends of the kernels remain attached to the cob.

Using the blunt side of the knife (the opposite side of the blade), gently scrape down the length of the cob to extract the milk and the rest of the kernels. Six ears of corn will yield approximately 2 cups of kernels.

Preparing Fresh Greens

Cut the tough ribs or stems and any yellow or bruised leaves from the greens and discard. Gently rub the front and the back of the leaves with your fingers under warm running water to remove any dirt or debris until clean. Roll several leaves together into a tube shape. Cut the tube into 1/2-inch sections to form strips. Let the strips soak in warm, salted water for 10 minutes, changing the water three or four times to rinse away grit and dirt. Rinse with cool water and drain in a colander.

Preparing Fresh Mushrooms

To clean fresh mushrooms, wipe them with a damp cloth or a paper towel. Do not rinse, soak, or wash them because it increases their water content. Keep them cool and dry. Refrigerate them in a basket or an open paper bag. They should stay fresh for 1 to 2 days.

Blanching Vegetables

A large pot with a strainer basket works best, but if you don't have one, a large colander will stand in nicely.

Wash the vegetables. Bring a pot of water to a boil. Add a teaspoon of salt to the water. Place the vegetables in the hot water for 4 to 6 minutes. Plunge the vegetables into a bowl of ice water to stop the cooking process and retain the color.

Toasting Nuts and Seeds

Toasting nuts and seeds intensifies their flavor. To dry-toast them on the stove top, place a single layer of nuts or seeds in a dry skillet over medium-low heat and cook, shaking the pan often, for 2 to 3 minutes, or until fragrant. Remove from the heat and stir until they cool slightly and emit a pronounced toasted aroma. You can also dry-toast them in a 300-degree oven on a baking sheet for 5 to 15 minutes, depending on the size of the nuts.

BASIC RECIPES

If you're feeling adventurous, give these homemade ingredients a try. Make the ones you think you'll use the most, and keep them on hand to use at a moment's notice. You'll love the results and, most of all, the sweet satisfaction of having created your very own fresh ethnic vegetarian ingredients.

1-2-3 VEGETABLE BROTH

MAKES 8 CUPS

8   cups water
5   ribs celery, quartered
3   carrots, quartered
2   large yellow onions, peeled and quartered
1   leek, trimmed and quartered
7   black peppercorns
6   cloves garlic, peeled
4   bay leaves
    Sea salt

Place the water in a large pot over high heat. Add the celery, carrots, onions, leek, peppercorns, garlic, bay leaves, and salt to taste. Bring to a boil. Reduce the heat to low and simmer for 20 minutes. Remove from the heat and allow the broth to cool.

Strain the broth into an airtight container. Discard the vegetables. Chill the broth in the refrigerator.

RICH VEGETABLE BROTH

MAKES 7 CUPS

1   cup (about 1 ounce) dried porcini mushrooms
6   cups hot water
1½   teaspoons unsalted butter
½   teaspoon vegetable oil
4   shallots, coarsely chopped
1   garlic clove, peeled and crushed
1   cup Madeira wine
1   bay leaf
2   tablespoons soy sauce

Soak the mushrooms in the hot water in a large bowl for 20 minutes, or until soft. Set aside.

Melt the butter in a large saucepan over medium heat. Add the oil, shallots, and garlic. Reduce the heat to low, cover, and cook for 5 minutes, stirring frequently, or until the shallots are golden brown. Add the Madeira and increase the heat to high. Bring to a boil and boil for 3 minutes, or until the liquid is reduced by half. Reduce the heat to low.

Carefully pour the mushrooms and soaking liquid into the saucepan, using almost all of the liquid except the portion that contains the grit at the bottom of the bowl. Add the bay leaf and soy sauce and gently simmer the broth for 30 minutes. Pour the broth through a fine sieve into an airtight container. Refrigerate for no more than 3 days.

GARLIC-TOFU MAYONNAISE

MAKES 1 CUP

4   cloves garlic, peeled
1   teaspoon salt
3   green onions, white parts only
4   ounces soft, silken tofu, drained
⅓   cup extra-virgin olive oil
¼   cup water
2   tablespoons freshly squeezed lemon juice
2   teaspoons Dijon mustard
1   teaspoon lemon zest
1   teaspoon freshly ground black pepper

Place the garlic and salt in a food processor and process into a paste. Add the green onions and blend for 1 minute. Add the tofu, oil, water, lemon juice, mustard, lemon zest, and pepper. Blend until smooth. Place in an airtight container and refrigerate.

Cooking Tip: If you want to make plain tofu mayonnaise, just omit the garlic.

VEGETARIAN WORCESTERSHIRE SAUCE

MAKES 3 CUPS

- 1 large yellow onion, peeled and quartered
- 3 teaspoons yellow mustard seeds
- 2 cloves garlic, peeled and crushed
- 1 slice (1¼ inches) ginger
- 1 piece (1 inch long) cinnamon stick
- 1 teaspoon black peppercorns
- 1 teaspoon cloves
- ½ teaspoon red-pepper flakes
- ½ teaspoon cardamom pods
- 2 cups white wine vinegar
- ½ cup molasses
- ½ cup soy sauce
- ¼ cup tamarind pulp
- ½ cup water
- 3 tablespoons salt
- ½ teaspoon curry powder

Place the onion, mustard seeds, garlic, ginger, cinnamon stick, peppercorns, cloves, red-pepper flakes, and cardamom in the middle of a large square of cheesecloth. Gather up the edges of the cheesecloth tightly and tie a piece of kitchen string around the top to make a bag. Place the bag of spices, the vinegar, molasses, soy sauce, and tamarind pulp in a large saucepan. Bring to a boil over high heat. Reduce the heat to low and simmer for 45 minutes.

Combine the water, salt, and curry powder in a small bowl. Stir into the mixture in the saucepan. Remove the sauce from the heat.

Place the sauce and the spice bag in a stainless steel or glass container. Cover tightly and refrigerate. For the next 2 weeks, mix the sauce occasionally and squeeze the liquid out of the spice bag. After 2 weeks, remove and discard the spice bag. Keep the Worcestershire sauce refrigerated, tightly covered, and mix before using.

Cooking Tip: Commercially prepared Worcestershire sauces use anchovies for flavoring. This is a vegetarian version. It calls for tamarind pulp, which is available in many Asian and East Indian markets.

ITALIAN SEASONING MIX

MAKES ABOUT 1 CUP

- **2** tablespoons dried basil
- **2** tablespoons dried oregano
- **2** tablespoons dried parsley
- **2** tablespoons dried sage
- **2** tablespoons dried rosemary
- **2** tablespoons dried thyme leaves
- **2** tablespoons ground marjoram
- **2** tablespoons celery seed

Combine the basil, oregano, parsley, sage, rosemary, thyme, marjoram, and celery seed in an airtight container. Shake well and store in a cool, dry place.

SEITAN

MAKES 1¼ POUNDS

- **2** cups whole wheat gluten flour
- **1** teaspoon salt
- **1** teaspoon onion powder
- **1** teaspoon garlic powder
- **½** teaspoon white pepper
- **1** cup water
- **1** cup plain soy milk

Combine the flour, salt, onion powder, garlic powder, and pepper in a large bowl. Add the water and soy milk. Mix the ingredients together with a fork to form a thick, stiff dough.

Knead the dough with your hands 10 to 15 times. Let the dough rest for 5 minutes. Knead it again about 6 to 8 times. Place it in a bowl, cover with a clean kitchen towel, and allow to rest in a warm, draft-free place for 15 minutes. The seitan is now ready to be cooked. Or place it in a container of water, cover tightly, and refrigerate, or place in a plastic bag and freeze.

Cooking Tip: To make chicken-flavored seitan, add 2 tablespoons of poultry seasoning to the flour and omit the onion powder and garlic powder.

INDEX

Underscored page references indicate cooking tips.

Conversion Chart

These equivalents have been slightly rounded to make measuring easier.

Volume Measurements

U.S.	Imperial	Metric
¼ tsp	–	1 ml
½ tsp	–	2 ml
1 tsp	–	5 ml
1 Tbsp	–	15 ml
2 Tbsp (1 oz)	1 fl oz	30 ml
¼ cup (2 oz)	2 fl oz	60 ml
⅓ cup (3 oz)	3 fl oz	80 ml
½ cup (4 oz)	4 fl oz	120 ml
⅔ cup (5 oz)	5 fl oz	160 ml
¾ cup (6 oz)	6 fl oz	180 ml
1 cup (8 oz)	8 fl oz	240 ml

Weight Measurements

U.S.	Metric
1 oz	30 g
2 oz	60 g
4 oz (¼ lb)	115 g
5 oz (⅓ lb)	145 g
6 oz	170 g
7 oz	200 g
8 oz (½ lb)	230 g
10 oz	285 g
12 oz (¾ lb)	340 g
14 oz	400 g
16 oz (1 lb)	455 g
2.2 lb	1 kg

Length Measurements

U.S.	Metric
¼"	0.6 cm
½"	1.25 cm
1"	2.5 cm
2"	5 cm
4"	11 cm
6"	15 cm
8"	20 cm
10"	25 cm
12" (1')	30 cm

Pan Sizes

U.S.	Metric
8" cake pan	20 × 4 cm sandwich or cake tin
9" cake pan	23 × 3.5 cm sandwich or cake tin
11" × 7" baking pan	28 × 18 cm baking tin
13" × 9" baking pan	32.5 × 23 cm baking tin
15" × 10" baking pan	38 × 25.5 cm baking tin (Swiss roll tin)
1½ qt baking dish	1.5 liter baking dish
2 qt baking dish	2 liter baking dish
2 qt rectangular baking dish	30 × 19 cm baking dish
9" pie plate	22 × 4 or 23 × 4 cm pie plate
7" or 8" springform pan	18 or 20 cm springform or loose-bottom cake tin
9" × 5" loaf pan	23 × 13 cm or 2 lb narrow loaf tin or pâté tin

Temperatures

Fahrenheit	Centigrade	Gas
140°	60°	–
160°	70°	–
180°	80°	–
225°	105°	¼
250°	120°	½
275°	135°	1
300°	150°	2
325°	160°	3
350°	180°	4
375°	190°	5
400°	200°	6
425°	220°	7
450°	230°	8
475°	245°	9
500°	260°	–